Shadow
of the
OhshaD

Claire,
    Pleasure working with you
Hope you this collection
    of lore, nature, Indians,
gunfighters and wicked women

By Gary Every

Shadow of the OhshaD

Tales from The Oracle

The Oracle newspaper
is proud to present the best
Arizona Adventures
from award-winning author
Gary Every

International Standard Book Number
978-0-615-30343-7

Published by
The Oracle
Oracle, Arizona 85623 USA

Book design and production by Kate Horton
Cover jaguar photo: courtesy Arizona Game & Fish Dept.
See photo / art credits: Page 262

Printed in the United States of America

To
my mom Carol Maki, my dad John Every,
and my birth mom

Table of Contents

Introduction

Gary Every is a very prolific writer. I don't know how he finds time to go on his adventures and do his research while working full time. He usually works at resorts where, in addition to his regular duties, he entertains guests with his unusual tales.

Gary has been writing stories and poems for *The Oracle* newspaper for almost ten years. This book is a collection of those articles. He has published several other books of his work and has sold stories to many other publications.

This talented writer is also an actor. He is available to entertain groups with programs based on his work. Sometimes a friend will accompany him on the flute.

Every writes about many subjects, but his passion is the jaguar or The OhshaD. He dreams of a day when the jaguar returns to Arizona. The jaguar is a large spotted feline of tropical America. It is similar to the leopard. On very rare occasions, one might be seen this side of the Mexican border.

While he travels the Arizona desert on his adventures, Gary is always hoping to see The OhshaD.

– Ellie Mattausch
Editor and publisher of
The Oracle

chapter 1:
Shadow of the OhshaD

The one journey I really wish to take is a stroll along the Sendero Pantera – the panthers' path. El camino gato grande is a series of Central American highways designed to allow predator felines to travel from mountain range to mountain range. Environmentalists wish to stretch the Sendero Pantera from Guatemala to Greenland so that the Aztec panther can consort with his Florida cougar cousins or meet a nice Vancouver mountain-lion mama.

I imagine the Sendero Pantera is traveled by wild kitties of all sizes, shapes, stripes, and spots; including bobcat, magyar, jaguar, and ocelot. I want to stroll the Sendero Pantera and hunt for jaguar. I want to discover a feline Mayan-highland prince and convince him to follow me home to the Arizona Sonoran Desert where jaguars once lived. So that, once more, the walnut trees will be crowned with fierce, growling ghosts of spot and shadow.

The last jaguar killed in Arizona placed a curse upon us all; even killing Santa Claus. After being trapped in Campo Bonito, the last jaguar's pelt was given as a Christmas gift to William Cody. The original Buffalo Bill of the Wild West show used to dress up as Santa Claus to entertain the Oracle schoolchildren.

On a warm desert-winter Christmas day, the exact same day that Buffalo Bill was given the jaguar pelt, William Cody overheated in his Santa Claus suit, caught chill, then pneumonia, and eventually died. Neither a jaguar nor an authentic Santa Claus has been spotted in Arizona since.

I want to travel the Sendero Pantera and bring some jaguars back. There is an ancient word for them just waiting to be used. *OhshaD is* the Hohokam name for the jaguar.

I want the jaguar to return to my homeland even though some of them will turn out to be were-jaguars who can change themselves into mischievous, evil, little boys on full-moon nights. I want to fill the forests with fierce, spotted ghosts, forcing hikers to watch and listen for silent, stalking death. I want to fill the moonlit slopes with were-jaguars who will wreak havoc, mischief, and murder so that humans will learn to tremble once more at the shadow of the OhshaD. People might have a little more respect for the earth if they remembered how to be afraid of the forest again.

chapter 2:
Incinerator Ridge

The geology of southern Arizona is considered a classic example of basin-and-range topography. The mountains which tower above the valley floors have come to be called "sky islands" by environmentalists and naturalists. These sky islands provide ecosystems and habitats vastly different from those found on the desert floor. Best of all, sky islands provide refuge from the summer heat.

One of these refuges can be found north of Tucson in the pine forests of the Santa Catalina Mountains. Recently, a friend and I went hiking on Incinerator Ridge. My friend used to camp there in his Boy Scout days. He underwent a most unusual ritual there, a rite of passage he has never forgotten.

We turned off the main highway and onto the short dirt road which led to the trail head. Incinerator Ridge is located near the top of Mt. Lemmon, where stiff breezes provide a welcome relief from the stifling heat of an Arizona summer. As we walk along the trail we see several rings of rocks and other remnants of recent large fires.

My friend recalled the huge bonfires his Boy Scout troops used to build there while camping overnight. The cooling breezes become quite strong at night, stiff winds fan the flames of the large fires and make the blazes leap higher. It is Smoky the Bear's worst nightmare. We begin to notice the large number of giant charred tree trunks and burnt-wood carcasses that are littered all around us. This trail is known as Incinerator Ridge for good reason.

The trail is not long, mildly steep and, at 8,000 feet in elevation, provides a wonderful escape from the summer heat on the desert floor. The rock ledge vista provides a nice view of Rose Canyon Lake below. The trail junction gives hikers several options, including a long steep slope which drops down the north face at a rapid rate. A faint, ancient trail leads to a miner's shack besides a natural spring with a wonderful vista of the surrounding countryside. The cabin has collapsed. Only a little further down the trail is the mine where the prospector was working.

Located near the entrance to the mine shaft is an iron wheelbarrow that no one has had the gumption to haul back up the steep cliff face. In the mine shaft, my friend discovers an old candleholder with a knife blade welded onto it. This tool allowed the miner to stick the knife into one of the mine-shaft timbers and leave the prospector with both hands free to work.

As we stand on the grounds of the old Boy Scout Camp, my friend marvels at the old stone wall. It is funny how nostalgic memories can sometimes play tricks. My friend vividly remembers camping here as a little scout, amidst the boulders and pines. He does not remember a large stone wall or a level campground. He only remembers the feeling of braving the untamed wilderness on an overnight trip with his comrades and friends.

He begins to recount the nature of his secret Incinerator Ridge initiation to me. The Fire Master built a roaring bonfire while my friend and all the other young campers pulled in close to the flames. They were sitting right up against the fire to take the chill off their backs as the stiff breezes raced up the steep mountain slopes. The boys had been informed that they were not supposed to speak during the ceremony. The Fire Master explained that the boys would all undergo a ritual of initiation; an early test of their emerging manhood.

The Drum Master sat beside the Fire Master and began a slow and steady drum beat as the initiates were taught the secret chant. Each syllable is long and drawn out, the vowels are held for a long time, almost like a Buddhist chant. The boys would speak in unison, loudly repeating the strange sounds of the Fire Master as he spoke with his eyes closed. As the drum beat steadily but slowly, the echoes of the boys voices begin to fill the forest night.

The sacred, secret chant of Incinerator Ridge, the first words the boys were allowed to speak at the campfire, goes like this: *"O Wa Ta Goo Sigh Am."* The drums kept beating and the boys kept chanting, louder and louder. My friend says that it seemed like they chanted all night, for hours and hours. The voices cried out, *"O Wa Ta Goo Sigh Am."* The Fire Master kept throwing more logs onto the fire, making the blaze burn further and further, higher and higher, into the midnight hours.

My friend said the rules of the initiation were quite simple. The initiates were required to repeat the sacred secret chant over and over until they had divined its mystery. When an initiate had deciphered the secret chant he would approach the Drum Master and whisper the secret into the Drum Master's ear. If the initiate was correct then he would leave the fire and join the elders while they waited and watched.

"O Wa Ta Goo Sigh Am."

Go ahead. Try to repeat the chant yourself and see how quickly you can decipher the mysterious meaning. I will give you a hint. It helps to repeat the words more quickly so that they run together. Then you can easily hear the alternative spelling.

The alternative spelling of the secret sacred chant looks like this: "O What A Goose I Am."

The Apache Naichee ceremonies feature the "Sponsor Dance" (top) and the "Corn Pollen Blessing" (above).

chapter 3:
The Apache Naichee Ceremony

The most important of Apache rituals is the Naichee ceremony, the female puberty initiation. Four days of pageantry include drumming, dancing, singing, and rituals to bless both the initiate and the community. Feathers, seashells, cattail pollen, and the observers all play important roles in the colorful Naichee ceremony.

For many years, the Naichee ceremony was banned by the Army. This religious censorship lasted for decades. Even today, the cost and time commitment of the ritual prohibits many families from taking part. In his book *Cibecue Apache*, Keith Basso writes of one father waffling back and forth on the matter.

"I wasn't sure of having a dance. My wife wanted to because she had one when she was a girl. Now some people think it is old fashioned and the medicine men don't have the power. It costs a lot too. We don't know what to do. Then it came close to when my daughter was to bleed for the first time, so we had to get going.

"My mother came to my camp and said, 'I hear you won't give my granddaughter Naichee. Why don't you have her one? I am an old lady but I am still strong. Naichee did that.' We decided it was good to have one."

One of the central participants in the ritual is the sponsor, a respected woman of the community who serves a role similar to a godmother. This woman must not be related by clan and must possess sterling qualities such as strength of character, intelligence, courage, and a sense of humor. At one point in the ceremony, the sponsor massages the young girl as if she is molding pottery; as if she is shaping a vessel which will hold all the qualities of divine femininity.

The abalone shell the girl wears upon her forehead is symbolic of this divinity, representing the sea shell upon which the great Apache goddess known as White Changing Woman floated during the Great Flood. During the course of this four-day ceremony, aided by the blessings of her community, the power of the medicine man, and her own ability to endure the rigorous ordeal, the young girl will transform into the holy person White Changing Woman for a short time.

Another important character in the ceremony is the shaman or medicine man. When the father has selected a medicine man to sing for his daughter, he must journey on foot to the medicine man's house and arrive before sunrise with a traditional payment of cash, eagle feathers, turquoise, and cattail pollen. The medicine man will sing songs of magic and power intended to instruct and transform the young girl.

I have never seen a Naichee ceremony where the young girl did not look beautiful. She wears the abalone shell pendant atop her forehead and her long black silky hair is combed back with a gray or white eagle feather hanging down from the braid. Legends say that the young girl will live a long life until her hair turns the color of the eagle feather. She wears a beautiful buckskin serape covered with handmade bead work and a lengthy fringe hanging from the sleeves so her arms move like wings while she is dancing.

At one point in the ceremony the medicine man will attach two small feathers of eagle down to the girl's shoulders so that she might walk and run as lightly as feathers float on air. Probably the most important item in her attire is the cane. The cane is decorated with bells to make it jangle while she dances. It is adorned with eagle feathers for a long life and oriole feathers for a good disposition. She will keep this cane throughout her life. It is the cane she will lean upon in old age.

In late summer of 2002 a Naichee ceremony was held on the San Carlos Reservation in the tiny town of Peridot. I left home in the dark in order to arrive at Peridot for the sunrise. The bright colors of the women's dresses shone in the morning light; blues, yellows, red, and turquoise. Many wear beautiful moccasin boots adorned with intricate beaded designs; suns, shields, and geometric patterns. Most of the women wear scarves with bright colors pinned to their breasts, many featuring American flags.

I am close enough to overhear one Apache elder boast that she has brought five generations of Apache females to this dance to help bless this young initiate. The beautiful face of this old woman is reflected again and again in the generations of the girls surrounding her. From matriarch to great-great-granddaughter, their resemblance is remarkable.

In his book, *The People*, author Stephen Trimble relates an Apache anecdote: Women are the trunk of the family tree, children the branches, and husbands the leaves. Traditionally, sisters and daughters live together forever and men enter the family only through marriage. The Apache say that, "The leaves may drop off, but the trunk and branches will never break."

In the Trimble book there is an accompanying photo of a beautiful Apache maiden whose piercing smile reminds me of my Sioux friend, Nelson, who left his Montana reservation to come to Arizona because his favorite uncle had always told him that Apache women were the most beautiful women in the world.

These women at the Peridot ceremony dance in their brightly colored dresses and are more than just observers, they are participants as well. Lining up in two long rows facing each other, the women lock arms and dance in place for much of the ceremony. Their shuffling feet, singing voices, and good hearts all contribute to the blessings they are offering the young girl.

The two rows of brightly clothed women face each other while the sponsor and the initiate stand side by side. The musicians stand behind the sponsor and young girl, drums in the crooks of their arms as the one hand flails a steady beat. The shaman stands at the front of the musicians and sings of melody and magic.

The shaman at the Peridot ceremony is dressed more like a cowboy than the stereotypical Hollywood Indian. Many of the men are wearing cowboy clothing; ten-gallon hats, boots, flannel shirts, and blue jeans. Most of the boys wear the athletic logos of their favorite sports teams. New Mexico Lobos and Arizona Wildcats are prominent among them.

Flanking the band in a thin line stretching either way are male relatives of the girl. They dance proudly, jangling the bells hanging beneath their baskets. These uncles, cousins, brothers, dance with high steps and arms constantly moving, knowing that it is their love and energy that will aid the young girl. The drums continue to pound as the medicine man sings his mesmerizing chant, and I bounce to the beat until my calf muscles grow weary.

It is a beautiful day and I am happy to be here. I was unable to attend the first Naichee I received an invitation for. It was about five years previous and I was coming home from a trout-fishing expedition. On my drive home I was taking the scenic route across the White Mountain Reservation when I pulled into the prehistoric ruins at Kinnishba.

The Mogollon peoples inhabited Kinnishba well over 1,000 years ago. Kinnishba is an Apache word which means brown, brick house. The ruins were partially restored by the University of Arizona as they tried to build the Apache a

Mesa-Verde-style tourist trap. The museum-gift shop burned down while the ruins were only one-third restored and the entire project was abandoned.

To reach Kinnishba you follow a dirt road to a fork splitting into two smaller dirt roads. A small, hand-painted sign reads "Kinnishba, Holy Ground" and two arrows point to the left. The restored portions of the ruins are slowly crumbling back into the earth while the burned out shell of the museum sits perched atop the hill. There are tree limbs poking in and out of windows and the whole feeling is pretty spooky.

Kinnishba contains an interior courtyard where one is surrounded by the beautiful red-brick architecture. It was here that archaeologists found a stone altar. The altar was painted with a crowned dancer who was surrounded by cornstalks and lightning bolts. The Apache do not claim to be direct descendants of the Mogollon. They claim that Kinnishba was abandoned because those people who once lived here forgot their Gods.

One day while visiting Kinnishba, I was scanning the archaeology trash mounds and admiring the beautiful stripes and colors of the pottery, when a pickup truck approached and pulled in beside my weather-beaten economy car. The truck belonged to an Apache father who had come here with an eagle feather and an invitation for the Gods who once resided here. An invitation to his daughter's Naichee. He decides that I am supposed to attend as well. He hands me an invitation on bright yellow paper.

Apache Naichee Ceremony invitation

I am grateful to attend the ceremony at Peridot on a warm

21

day filled with sunshine and good blessings. It is a chance to finally redeem a lost obligation. When everybody else dances, I dance too. I bob in place and wiggle my arms slightly, captured by the bands rhythmic beat. I close my eyes, lost in the shaman's song, words chanted in a language I don't understand, chorus repeated by the band. I dance some more, bouncing up and down on my toes until my legs grow tired. Then I dance some more, feeling warm and protected by the sunshine. Purification through dancing is a beautiful concept.

It is amazing that the young girl can dance for so long. The buckskin serape looks very warm and heavy as the summer sun climbs. The girl grows close to overheating. Then she dances some more. There are parts of the ceremony where the sponsor and the young girl dance, parts where just the women dance, parts where everyone dances, but the young girl is the only one who dances continuously. She hops lightly from one foot to the other while the fringe on her serape waves in the breeze like wings. During the ceremony she is expected to fast and the only liquid she can consume must be sipped through a straw made from a hollow cattail-plant stalk.

I speak with one Apache woman who says that as the trials and tribulations of life arrive to visit her, she always reminds herself of the physical ordeal which purified her during the Naichee ceremony. If she had the strength to endure all that dancing then surely she has the strength for anything.

Her cane is involved in one of the most important rituals. The medicine man and the sponsor take the cane and walk to the east, planting the cane in the ground. The sponsor stands beside it while the young girl runs out beyond the cane and then back to her original place. This is supposed to symbolize her ability to surpass and go beyond the obstacles in her life.

Then the medicine man moves the cane a little further away. The young girl runs again and this time all the woman and children follow. Then the medicine man places the cane even further away and now everybody follows the girl.

Next, the men form a line and approach the young girl reverently with a pinch of cattail pollen between their fingers. The men approach and each offers a blessing such as a long life, luck in love, good education, or many children. In turn, they can ask for a blessing themselves. They sprinkle a few grains of cattail pollen atop her head. As the line passes through, the pollen makes her begin to glow as if she is made of gold.

The women come next with more pinches of pollen between their fingertips. Sometimes, as a particularly respected female approaches, the medicine man will stop and have the girl massage this matriarch so that all the elder's good qualities will pass into the young girl. Babies are presented to the initiate, so that in her temporary transformation into White Changing Woman she can hold the babies up to face each of the four directions and bless them.

The Naichee ends with the rows of women and men breaking into smaller family units which lock arms while approaching and retreating from the young girl. The young woman dances with her hands raised up pointing towards the heavens. The small groups of people surround and gradually close in on the girl as they approach and retreat with locked arms. They press in on all sides, dancing and singing; the entire village welcoming the young girl into the community as an adult.

As she dances in her beautiful serape, adorned with eagle and oriole feathers, abalone shell atop her forehead, and hair glistening gold with pollen, she does indeed look every bit the White Changing Woman. While the community welcomes and blesses her, she blesses all of them in her temporary transformation as a holy woman. As a symbol of theses abundant riches, the shaman over turns a basket atop her head. The basket is filled with acorns, candy, fruit, and coins. As all these goodies spill on the ground the children scramble and wrestle for the loot, their giggling laughter echoing off the Peridot Hills.

chapter 4:
The Gardens of Gethsemane

Located along the Santa Cruz Riverpark in Tucson, Arizona, is one of the most sacred places in the city – Gethsemane Gardens. The Riverpark follows the winding serpentine banks of the arroyo. The paved pathways serve walkers, joggers, bicyclists, and rollerblade enthusiasts; Gethsemane Gardens provides sanctuary for many of these Riverpark enthusiasts.

Gethsemane Gardens can be found where the Santa Cruz River intersects the St. Mary's Road on the north side of the pavement. Surrounded by a fenced enclosure and a tall stand of bamboo, this green garden is one of the best places in the city to sit, read, and listen to the choruses of birds harmonizing in the green foliage.

Gethsemane Gardens is a shrine dedicated to the works of local sculptor Felix Lucero. His religious statues decorate the park. Lucero possessed no academic or technical training yet his statues, including a life-size depiction of the Last Supper, the Virgin Mother, the Crucifixion, and various saints, are praised for technical precision and detail. For example, one can make out the outline of individual coins in the bag sitting beside Judas in the Last Supper sculpture.

The statues were the result of a battlefield promise made during World War I. As a young soldier, frightened and far from home, Felix Lucero was trapped in a no man's land on a French battlefield. All his superior officers had been killed and he had nearly given up hope. Then Lucero saw a vision of a 40-foot tall Jesus forming in the smoke above the battlefield. He made a promise to God that if he survived he would dedicate his life to holy works. Lucero led himself and nine other soldiers to safety, receiving medals, honors, and commendations for his acts of bravery.

One time while bicycling along the Riverpark for some exercise, I paused to catch my breath, take a drink from a water fountain and partake of some solitude in Gethsemane Gardens. A craftsman was there that day repairing some heartless vandal's damage to the statues. It seems the garden attracts the occasional crackpot who comes intent on damaging the statues. Although they never attack in concert, they usually only destroy Christ's extremities, smashing noses, toes, and fingers. While I was observing the craftsman as he was repairing Christ's fingers, he explained to me how he had to be careful and precise. It is not just a matter of duplicating Lucero's technical skills, but also his vision. The hands, he told me, must hold strength, wisdom, love, joy, and forgiveness. The hands, he said, must hold the tenderness of heaven's embrace. He carefully crafted and resculpted the fingers, trying to get them just right.

After World War I, when Felix Lucero returned to Tucson, he lived in a shack beneath the old Congress Street bridge. He kept the promise he made during the heat of the battle in France and built statues of sand in the river bottom. He meticulously carved life-size statues of religious figures and scenes which would wash away during every monsoon or winter soaking. Felix Lucero would then leave his shack beneath the bridge and build more sculptures.

He did this for decades and, as time passed, he became a neighborhood legend. There was the tale of a drunken man on horseback who was riding along the Santa Cruz River one day and came upon Lucero while he was working. The drunken man ridiculed the statues before trampling them beneath his horse's hooves. According to the legend, further down the wash, a rattlesnake spooked the horse. It reared up and tossed the rider, breaking his neck.

Jim Griffith, the folklorist who told me that tale, said that such stories show what an integral part of the neighborhood identity Lucero and his statues had become. In the late 1940s, when Lucero's shack beneath the Congress Street bridge burned down, the community showed just how important he was by raising funds to put Lucero and his wife into an apartment. They also contributed money to pay for the labor and materials for the statues which currently stand in the park.

Detail of "The Last Supper" sculpture from the Gardens of Gethsemane

All the materials in Gethsemane Gardens were harvested from the Santa Cruz, from the sand for the plaster to the abandoned box-spring mattress which comprises the table of the Last Supper sculpture. Even Judas' 30 pieces of silver are made from scavenged coins discovered along the river bottom.

The garden is frequented by photographers. Some come to take pictures of the statues, birds, or the soft interplay of light as it filters down through the thick branches of foliage.

The last time I was shutterbugging there I lost myself in the lens and failed to notice a transient who entered the enclave. He stood beside my unlocked bicycle and bookpack which contained my wallet, bank card, credit cards, and personal I.D. The transient nodded a polite hello and waited patiently for me to finish taking pictures. I had no idea how long he had been standing there but he could have stolen my things long before I noticed him. I finished quickly and, as I approached, he cleared his throat to speak with me, somewhat shyly, perhaps awed with a reverence for this place. Then he asked me for spare change.

Perhaps because he did not steal my things when he could have, or perhaps because the very nature of this place made me feel charitable, I gave him two dollars. As he thanked me, his trembling hands reached for the money. I was startled to realize that his hands had no fingers.

chapter 5:
El Dias De Los Muertos or Day of the Dead

One Halloween I loaded myself into my automobile and headed south towards the international border. I wanted to be in Mexico to observe and photograph the holiday known as *El Dias De Los Muertos* or Day of the Dead. Starting with Halloween on October 31, there is a series of three holidays. November 1 is All Saint's Day in the Catholic faith. November 2 is the Mexican holiday known as The Day of the Dead. *El Dias De Los Muertos* is a unique mixture of Catholic and Mesoamerican Indian beliefs.

On Halloween I had been shooting seasonal pictures, taking photographs of my friend William Cole's 12-foot-long Colombian boa, Vixen, as she slithered amongst my skull collection. Yes, I have a skull collection. While hiking, when I find deer, fox, or javelina skulls, I collect them. The pictures of the snakes came out great.

I was making my living as a chef at the time. I threw my cameras, skulls, and chefs-knife bag into the trunk before driving south from Tucson on Interstate 19, following the line of missions towards the border.

First comes San Xavier de Bac, then Tubac, Tumacoccari, and Guevavi; remnants of the Spanish historical legacy. I entered Mexico in the border town of Nogales. I change countries, from the U.S. to Mexico, just by crossing a fence. I change countries but I do not change cities. I am still in Nogales.

Nogales is a Spanish word meaning "walnut tree." Many trees grow along the wooded hillsides; walnut, oak, mesquite, and juniper. The landscape is composed of lush rolling hills, grasses and scrub forest.

Once I entered Mexico I followed the border fence across

the city, driving west. The only directions I have been given to find the cemetery were to follow the fence. I make a couple of wrong turns and met dead ends in neighborhoods. Slowly across the city, I followed the serpentine border fence. I came to sidewalks lined with vendors. I parked my car in front of the marketplace, figuring that I can shop from stall to stall and perhaps receive directions to the cemetery. As soon as I open the car door and step outside I realize the vendors have lined up along the sidewalks surrounding the cemetery. The fiesta takes place in the graveyard itself. I have discovered the *Panteon Nacional*.

There are several stalls selling religious pendants, statues and medallions. The wonderful smells of taco stands fill the chill autumn air with the aromas of warm, spicy food. Several stalls in a row sell flowers, brilliant colors exploding in the tiny spaces. The flower stalls sell carefully folded paper flowers, beautiful wreaths, irises, plastic roses, living yellow and white flowers, vines, and, of course, marigolds or *cempazuchiles*, the flower of the dead.

Men with sharp knives cut and prepare sugar cane. Boys walk the streets and sell sliced watermelon with salt and lime. It is delicious! So is the roasted corn. Other vendors sell manufactured goods such as pots and pans, music CDs, children's toys, rugs, and clothing. There are even places to buy tombstones and religious statues.

The cemetery itself is just like the city itself. The boneyard residents are crowded all across the hillsides. Every available space is filled. It is an egalitarian cemetery; the wealthy and impoverished lay here side by side. In death all men are equal; all that remains is a legacy of love.

This is the nature of the *El Dias Los Muertos* holiday. It is an occasion for the living to show respect for those they have lost. In the days leading up to The Day of the Dead the graveyards are filled with loving friends and family members; painting, cleaning, and decorating the graves.

Trash can shrine at Nogales, Mexico

Flowers are everywhere. The hillsides are filled with little clusters of bright flowers. There are bouquets and wreaths, clusters of picked flowers sitting in elaborate vases or resting in a small pool of water in the bottom of a coffee can. It all depends on the income of the loved ones. There are plastic flowers and living gardens. The colors are everywhere, including the yellow marigolds.

There are droves of religious statues. Many of the graves have some sort of statute ornamentation. These can range from tiny angels to life-size Messiahs. Some graves are adorned with sculptures of churches, with parapets which reach six-feet high. Many of the statues are hand painted; a sign of devotion which also lends traces of individuality to the graves.

The same angel statues are scattered all across the cemetery, but the sweet winged little girls frequently wear different colored dresses. The hairstyles of all the different Jesus are another matter. I saw the same Jesus-on-the-cross statue with different colors of hand-painted hair. There was white hair, black hair, brown hair, and a red-headed Jesus, as well as Messiah's wearing skins of black, white, and brown.

The cemeteries are a bustle of activity, filled with people fixing, cleaning, and decorating the graves of family members. Many parents come with young children in tow or babies carried in their arms; teaching the young to continue these ancient traditions. Some people work very hard. They include hired work crews with shovels, block, and concrete. The smell of wet paint is in the air; bright red, greens, yellows, and blues. Some graves are decorated with a variety of multi-colored flower petals strewn across the dirt; an Aztec aspect of the tradition.

Some people come only to exchange quiet conversations with lost loved ones.

The sidewalks are crowded with food, families, vendors, food, young people, more food, and references to the sacred. Buses come by regularly, always crowded. All day long the buses drop off and pick up people and they never seem to get more or less crowded. The same can be said for the herds of people on the sidewalks and wandering the cemetery. My small unit of tourists is nearly the only white faces we see all day. There is one man with an expensive camera and a long telephoto lens.

There is a change in the makeup of the crowd after nightfall. The families and the grandmothers disappear and are replaced by the smiling faces of young adults. There are hipsters, hustlers, and the romantically hopeful. This is the new Mexico.

Mexico is a nation where the predominant demographic is teenagers and young adults. It is these young people who will write the future of Mexico and perhaps leave a legacy in the U.S.

The nature of the fiesta changes as it gets darker and it becomes time to leave. I pull the car up to the customs station and impatiently wait my turn to speak with the U.S. agent. I roll down my window.

"Nature of business in Mexico?" the customs agents asks.

"Day of the Dead."

This captures the customs agent's attention. "You mean you came to Mexico just to visit the cemeteries?"

"Yes sir. I took lots of photographs."

"You came to Mexico just to photograph the cemeteries?" He shakes his head in disbelief. "I am afraid you will have to pull your automobile over into that spot over there and open the trunk for me."

So I did as I was told, knowing that the officer would open the trunk and discover the pile of skulls I had photographed along with the snake and the sharp bag of knives on top. It was the beginning of another story for another time.

Ak-Chin agriculture often features gourds.

chapter 6:
Ak-Chin Agriculture

The small brown man seated at the table is surrounded by huge green and yellow gourds. His ancient eyes stare into mine and he smiles. The smile looks handsome on a face worn and weathered by the sun.

This O'odham grandfather is sitting at a fair booth, explaining how his people have farmed in the deserts of southern Arizona for thousands of years. It is a style of agriculture based upon harvesting rain water known as Ak-Chin. The desert farmer is very proud of his big, beautiful, green and yellow gourds.

Corn was introduced to the region from Mexico in 2000 BC when the local inhabitants interrupted their hunting and gathering cycles for long enough to tend small gardens. Agriculture was only a supplement and not a mainstay until 750 BC when they bred an eight-row, 60-day popcorn and another popular strain known as *chapalote*.

Ethnobotanist Gary Paul Nabhan has collected ears of this 60-day popcorn still under cultivation in northern Mexico today. The agricultural lifestyle did not really explode in southern Arizona until the arrival of a culture we call the *Hohokam*.

The Hohokam were a group of astronomer priests who migrated from Mexico to rule the people already living in the area. The Hohokam brought several technological innovations with them. The first was pottery. When you store your food in baskets, the rats can chew through and eat your produce. A large pot can be sealed with beeswax and the food can be saved for a drought year. Farming in the southern Arizona desert, a region which averages only 8 to 12 inches of rain a year, holds the possibility of a drought year every year.

The Hohokam were master astronomers, keeping careful track of the best times to plant or harvest. These early scientists were also supreme genetic manipulators. What started out as a green weed called teosinte in Mesoamerica became 27 different varieties of corn being grown along the Salt River Basin by the time the Spanish arrived. Each variety was chosen for a different trait; flavor, durability, size, and even popping.

The small brown man at the O'odham Fair at Organ Pipe National Monument does not grow corn. He grows gourds, great big green and yellow gourds. They are the biggest squash I have ever seen, much bigger than acorn or butternut squash; twice the size of spaghetti squash.

The O'odham farmer has a small bowl of beans harvested from his farm. They are a type of tepary beans. In *The Desert Smells Like Rain*, Nabhan explains that farming with modern methods one can raise more pounds of beans per acre, but using ancient farming methods one raises more units of protein. It is the difference between farming for export or growing to feed your community.

This O'odham grandfather is keeping alive a style of dryland desert agriculture or *Ak-Chin*. Trying to farm amidst cactus thorns with summer temperatures above 100 degrees is no easy task. The real skill is the harvest of water. Ak-Chin farms are placed at the bottom of long gradual runoffs which stretch hundreds of miles all the way to mountain slopes in Mexico.

O'odham farmers use small stone dams, shallow trenches, reeds and grasses to slow down and capture the rain runoff. It is this skillfully engineered harvesting of rainwater which makes agriculture possible in this thirsty environment.

A woman standing beside me asks what the green and yellow gourds are called. We list several that we know but the O'odham man at the fair only smiles and nods. "I do not know the English name," he says. "I have never seen it in a grocery store." It is as big as a watermelon. The O'odham farmer says the vine has the same big orange yellow flowers as squash blossoms which grow in any garden anywhere. He says the huge gourds have a lot of meat in them and can provide dinner for three or four people after being baked in the oven with a little butter and a lot of cinnamon.

You should try growing watermelon, I tell him. "I do," he says. "The problem is the coyotes love to eat the watermelons. Every year I grow lots of watermelon and every year the coyotes come. This year I did not get to eat a single one, the coyotes got them all."

"You should put up a fence," the woman beside me advises.

"What are you going to do?" The O'odham farmer shrugs. "They are God's creatures too. If you want to keep any watermelons at all for yourself, then you must always be vigilant, even in the middle of the night. You have to be very ornery for a long time. I originally had many more squash than this." He pats a gourd lovingly, "But the javelinas ate most of them. Then, me and my wife ate most of the rest," he laughs while he rubs his belly.

He adds. "The quail will eat a lot of the squash if you are not careful."

"The quail can peck through the rinds with their stubby little beaks?" I ask.

He laughs. "They like the fresh sprouts when they are young and tender and have just erupted from the soil. One year my son was exasperated trying to chase the quail from the garden day after day, hour after hour, minute after minute. It had been a blessed year for rainfall. There were bean, watermelon, *chia*, and squash sprouts everywhere; sunflowers too but the quail were devastating, huge families of tiny quail babies following their mamas into the fields. It looked as if we might not have a harvest at all. Exasperated, my son grabbed the shotgun and ran into the field, shooting off just one blast, intending to scare away the quail for good."

"At sunset we heard a sad and plaintive cry. There sitting in the branches of an ironwood tree were the mother and father quail, calling to a lost baby. When we went into the fields, sure enough there was the dead body of a small fuzzy chick. I took the shotgun from my son and I said, 'God damn, we don't need this.'"

Sitting before the O'odham farmer are pictures of his land showing the preparation necessary to practice Ak-Chin agriculture. There are trenches to be dug, dams to be built, sticks and stones to be arranged. There is another photograph showing Baboquivari, the sacred peak of the O'odham, reflected in a shallow pool of water – the harvest of all that scientific engineering.

"There are no wells or springs or anything," someone says. "Is the amount of crops you raise totally determined by rainfall?"

"The amount of rainfall," he says, "And how much I pray . . . and why I pray. That is the most important part, why I pray."

He pauses to ponder and then tells me, "I farm because I like to hear the birds sing."

chapter 7:
The Lost Treasure of El Tejano

Most legendary of the southern Arizona stagecoach bandits was the outlaw known as *El Tejano*. El Tejano was probably the most picturesque of the local bad men; robbing stagecoaches all alone, armed only with a revolver in one hand and a bullwhip in the other, bands of bullets crisscrossing across his chest. El Tejano always robbed the stagecoaches with a smoldering cigar stuck between his lips, thick clouds of smoke rolling out from beneath his sombrero.

Although the name *El Tejano* translates literally from the Spanish language as "The Texan," most of the historical evidence suggests that he was really a suspected rustler from Missouri. Right from the start El Tejano became the stuff of legends. Perhaps it was because of the daring way he robbed the stagecoaches by himself.

El Tejano was all alone, except for hundreds of burros he brought with him. He used the burros to block the stagecoaches, trapping them in narrow canyons. He would herd hundreds of burros into a skinny mountain pass and the stagecoach driver would be forced to stop. When the robbery was over El Tejano used his bullwhip to scatter the burros; obscuring the hoof prints of his own escape.

Perhaps the reason for the quick growth of the El Tejano legend was that the amazing El Tejano never resorted to robbing passengers. This gave the outlaw a Robin-Hood persona. El Tejano never had to steal from the passengers because he only robbed stagecoaches that were laden with payrolls. This was by far the most lucrative type of highway robbery

After El Tejano had robbed ten stagecoaches laden with payrolls, the Wells Fargo Company gave up on their own security and the efforts of local law enforcement. Wells Fargo hired a Pinkerton agent to help solve the case. Pinkerton agents were held in the highest regard in the old west, sort of a whole Scotland Yard full of Sherlock Holmes. Juan Elias, Pinkerton agent, got off the train in Tucson and surveyed the scenery. He was met at the depot by the Wells Fargo station accountant, Bob Hand. Mr. Hand showed Mr. Elias to the inn where he had a room and helped him settle in. He wished the Pinkerton agent good night and good luck on capturing El Tejano in the morning. Juan Elias chuckled. He figured it would probably take longer than that to catch the outlaw bandit.

Mr. Elias was right about that. It took much longer. Four more stagecoach robberies occurred before the Pinkerton detective gathered his second clue. Four more stagecoach robberies by the cigar-chomping, sombrero-wearing, bullwhip-cracking, brazen El Tejano and Juan Elias knew he had better solve the case soon or start looking for another job. After the 14th robbery, Elias circled the scene of the crime, searching desperately for a clue, any sort of a clue.

And then he found it. In the dust was a set of horse hoof prints. The hooves did not belong to any of the steeds pulling the stagecoach so it must belong to El Tejano, he reasoned. It was a distinctive print too; the right forefoot shoe was missing two nails.

It was just the lucky break the Pinkerton agent needed to solve the case. The only problem was using his new piece of information. After every robbery, El Tejano would use his bullwhip to scatter his herd of burros and obliterate all other footprints in the process.

The Pinkerton agent needed to combine his two clues to solve the case. The first clue – if El Tejano only robbed stagecoaches with payrolls then he must have inside information. Somebody at Wells Fargo was telling El Tejano which stagecoaches to rob. Juan Elias went to the homes of all the Wells Fargo employees and searched for the distinctive hoof print he had noticed at the scene of the robberies. It took all of the day and most of the night, Elias would have had to abandon his search if it were not for the full moon which hung in the sky and illuminated his path.

The Pinkerton agent found the distinctive hoof print, missing the nails on the front shoe, belonging to the horse of El Tejano himself, outside the house of the least likely suspect.

The hoof print was outside the house of the accountant, Bob Hand. The Pinkerton agent never suspected for a moment that the frail, nervous, bespectacled accountant was really El Tejano, robbing stagecoaches all alone with a cigar and a bullwhip. Still, they were the only clues he had. Elias knew that if El Tejano robbed another payroll-laden stagecoach before he solved the case he would probably lose his job.

Elias decided to bluff. In the middle of the night, guided by the light of the full moon, the Pinkerton agent strolled to the front door of the accountant.

Knock-Knock.

"Who's there?" cried a timid voice.

"Juan Elias, Pinkerton agent. I have some questions for you Mr. Hand."

The accountant came to the door in his nightshirt, holding a candle and a feline.

Juan Elias explained his reason for coming, that he had

found a hoof print at the scene of the crime and that the investigative trail of that distinctive hoof print had led him to the door of Mr. Hand. Then Juan Elias played his bluff.

"You sir," Juan Elias poked his finger into the accountants skinny chest, "are really the bandit known as El Tejano!"

The accountant shrieked. His eyeglasses slipped from his head and while trying to adjust them he dropped both the candle and the cat.

"You sir, are under arrest."

"B-but it's not me. He forced me to tell him which stagecoaches were carrying payrolls. He is a mean man. You have no idea what a bully William Brazelton can be."

"Who?" Juan Elias asked, excited to finally have a name which he could associate with the legendary El Tejano.

William Brazelton was far from a legend but he was a well known figure in Territorial Tucson. He made regular appearances at the local saloons and had made quite a reputation for himself as a drunk, rogue, ruffian, and bully. William Brazelton had a ranch in the Tucson Mountains, along the slopes of Catback Mountain.

"W-W-William B-B-Brazelton," the accountant repeated nervously. "He said he would hurt me if I didn't tell him which stagecoaches were carrying payrolls."

"All you have to do," Juan Elias said, "is testify in court and we can lock up El Tejano for many years."

"T-T-testify?" Bob Hand stammered, "Oh, no! He is a mean man. You have no idea. He even threatened to shoot Mr. Whiskers." The accountant bent down and picked up his cat. "The wanted posters say Dead or Alive and you should definitely bring him back dead."

This presented Juan Elias with an ethical problem. If Bob Hand refused to testify the Pinkerton agent did not have much of a case. Most importantly, he needed more proof than just one man's word to kill another. The Pinkerton agent needed a plan. The next time a stagecoach was leaving Phoenix laden with a payroll, Elias telegraphed a request at the last minute to delay the trip by one day.

During that one day of delay, Juan Elias made an unexpected visit to the Brazelton ranch in the Tucson Mountains. He approached Mrs. Brazelton while she was hanging up laundry to dry.

"Excuse me ma'am . . . " Juan Elias said, "Is your husband home?"

"No," she replied, "He is away on business and won't be back for a few days."

"Of course, how stupid of me," the Pinkerton agent lied, "I saw him just yesterday up in Phoenix. He was walking out of a saloon. He was drunk as a skunk and he must have been gambling because money was dropping out of his pockets. He was staggering drunk, but it didn't matter because he was being supported on either arm by a painted lady."

"That son of a biscuit eater!" Mrs. Brazelton exclaimed. "He told me he was going up to Picacho to rob the stagecoach."

The tiny town of Picacho, Arizona, is famous for two points of trivial obscurity. The westernmost battle of the Civil War was fought here and Picacho is currently the home of the world's largest commercial ostrich farm.

The payroll-laden stagecoach rumbled toward the Picacho

station, approaching a narrow pass between two small hills. The driver suddenly found his way blocked by a large herd of burros. Chomping a foul-smelling cigar while the lash of his bullwhip circled the air, El Tejano waited for the stagecoach to arrive.

"Halt!" the bandit cried out.

The stagecoach stopped and, at that moment, the Pinkerton agent and the posse stepped out from their hiding places. They crept close to the waiting highwayman by sneaking amidst the herd of burros. The wanted posters said Dead or Alive and El Tejano was shot at point blank range by several shotguns.

It was customary in the Old West that, any time a figure of legendary notoriety was slain, the corpse was propped up in front of the courthouse for people to pay their respects or satisfy their curiosity. Many of the historical photographs we have of legendary outlaws were acquired in this way. William Brazelton was no exception and the only photograph of the outlaw known to exist is of his corpse, which has been propped up, holding a gun, and wearing a highwayman's mask to cover the disfiguring shotgun blast.

With that photograph of the bandit known as El Tejano, the historical trail ends but the stuff of legends and folklore just begins.

El Tejano robbed all these payrolls but the money was never recovered. After the death of her husband, his widow was too poverty stricken to keep up the ranch and abandoned it. Only the burros remained. Rumors began to spread and adventurers began to search for the lost treasure of El Tejano.

I remember as a youngster, burros roaming wild along the

slopes of the Tucson Mountains. The burros were removed decades ago by the park service when the area attained national-monument status but, according to the legends, one started a search for the treasure with the burros.

These burros were the descendants of El Tejano's herd. Once a treasure seeker had found the burros, he had to decide which of the beasts was El Tejano's favorite. El Tejano always loaded the bandit booty on to the back of his favorite burro and this burro remembered where the treasure was hidden. There are no clues on how to do this but once you have determined the favorite burro – follow this burro even if it takes all night.

When the wind blows the branches of the creosote bushes so fast that they begin to resemble the sound of a bullwhip cracking, look around.

There should be a cave or mine entrance near by. Except it is not really a cave or a mine, it is the beginning of a labyrinth. If one is lucky, really lucky, he or she tries to solve the maze, travels miles and miles underground, and comes out exactly where they started. If one is unlucky, they get lost and perish. The walls of El Tejano's labyrinth are said to be lined with the skeletons of the unfortunate lost.

However, if you are one of those people who have peculiar luck, you just might find yourself inside a large underground cavern, where smoky torches light the way. Glittering in the torch light, scattered upon the cavern floor, are the gold doubloons, silver pesos, and silver dollars that El Tejano stole from the payroll-laden stagecoaches.

It is then that the smell of cigar smoke fills the room. The ghost of El Tejano slowly materializes amidst the treasure; bullwhip first and then sombrero. His scowling mustache, covered with cigar ash, appears next, followed by his band of criss-crossing bullets and pistol, and finally, the torso.

When the ghost of El Tejano fully materializes, he speaks. He says only three words and they are in Spanish.

"Todo o nada."

All or nothing. He who cannot take the entire treasure, but only steals part of it, is cursed.

That is the trick. It is far more treasure than any one man can carry at one time. Some have resolved to leave the treasure alone and return when they are better prepared but they never find the cavern again. Others have been cursed.

I first heard the tale of El Tejano from my folklore professor at The University of Arizona, "Big" Jim Griffith. Griffith spoke of collecting oral histories from the Tucson's mostly Hispanic south side decades earlier.

Many Tucson families had claimed to have lost a favorite son, aunt, nephew or cousin who had seemed the picture of health but who had died mysteriously in their sleep the night after a long hike in the mountains. Always, a search of the dead person's clothing revealed a single old coin, gold or silver, but ancient – a piece of El Tejano's treasure.

Ordinarily, that would be the end of the story but not in the southwest where legends evolve and change as they are loved and adopted by different cultures.

During the first few decades of the 20th century, Mexico was a country of upheaval, revolution, and ethnic genocide. Much of the genocide was directed towards the Yaqui people. The Yaqui were a Native American people whose homeland for millennia was the valley of the Rio Yaqui several hundred miles to the south of the U.S. border.

To escape the violence and persecution, many Yaqui refugees fled north. There they formed small enclaves for economic survival and in an attempt to preserve some cultural continuity. Many of these new immigrants worked as ranch hands and railroad laborers in southern Arizona. They formed communities such as Barrio Pascua in Tucson and Barrio Guadalupe in Phoenix. During the Jimmy Carter administration, Yaqui reservations were established for this non-indigenous Native American group.

One of the largest Yaqui communities is outside Picacho, the town famous for the ostrich farm. Although El Tejano predates their arrival in this country the Yaqui have adopted him as a hero. The Yaqui versions of the tale have changed slightly from the original. The Yaqui tales expand upon the Robin Hood themes.

Located along the stretch of Interstate 10 between Tucson and Phoenix, the flat farm lands there are frequented by gusting winds. If you are driving this stretch of highway and suddenly a strong wind shakes your car, it is the ghost of El Tejano riding atop his invisible horse, charging down the slopes of Picacho Peak.

Since there are no more stagecoaches to rob, the highway bandit makes his money by shaking automobiles until the money between the seat cushions falls to the road.

In the Yaqui versions of the story it is possible to recover a piece of El Tejano's riches and live to tell the tale. Anyone who is hiking Picacho Peak State Park and feels a sudden gust of wind, should follow El Tejano's invisible horse as the legendary outlaw races back to his hideout. Treasure awaits the fleet of foot.

With this being the southwest, expect the legend of El Tejano to keep growing and changing as the centuries pass. I

47

hear that one of the Yaqui grandmothers is already telling the children that the ghost of El Tejano now charges down the slopes of Picacho Peak racing towards the automobiles atop his invisible ostrich.

chapter 8:
The 1887 Earthquake

The people of Tucson reported that, in the moments before the earthquake struck, all the stray dogs in town whined and trembled. Roosters crowed. Horses knelt. Even the chickens appeared nervous. It was May 3, 1887.

At the earthquake's epicenter near Bavispe, Mexico, the citizens of the sleepy town claimed that a low, rumbling, subterranean moan echoed through the hills about 15 minutes before catastrophe struck. The people of the town gathered inside the thick adobe walls of the Old Spanish mission. According to legend, all the citizens of Bavispe except three; the town drunk, the town harlot, and a mean, skeptical man of science, huddled inside the church praying.

The Apache, too, have legends concerning this earthquake. For years the Apache had been trying to capture a beautiful white stallion that ran wild along the shores of the San Pedro River. The wily mustang had eluded Apache lassos again and again, until one day the Apaches finally trapped their prey. The proud white stallion reared and whinnied as the painted Apache warriors approached. That is when the earthquake struck.

The earthquake is the largest to have ever struck Arizona in historical times, reaching an estimated 7.2 magnitude. Tremors were felt as far south as Mexico City and as far north as San Francisco. We know exactly what time the earthquake struck because all the pendulum clocks from Albuquerque to Globe and Phoenix were stopped by the swaying of the earth.

Interestingly enough, in the town of Las Cruces, New Mexico, the post office clock had been broken for nearly six months. The motion of the earth shook loose whatever was bothering the timepiece and the post office clock resumed keeping perfect time.

When the geological vibrations reached El Paso, Texas, shaking the Central School building, it caused one young lady to faint. One panicked lad leapt out a second story window. The house of Sheriff Texas John Slaughter in the San Bernadino Valley, crumbled into ruins. In Benson, Arizona, a Southern Pacific locomotive was dragged forward and back over the lines even though the parking brakes were set.

Miners working 400 feet beneath the earth in Bisbee were terrified as the shock waves rolled through the earth. The frightened men emerged only to discover that every mountain visible on the horizon had caught fire. At the train depot of Pantano, on the southern edge of the Rincon Mountains, a train nearly tumbled from a swaying trestle, teetering above the frightened town.

The residents of Charleston reported that nearly every building had been shaken and damaged. The walls of one local saloon did a two step and the floor did a shimmy. All the crumbled adobe filled the air with dust and created a veritable Kansas-style dust storm. Smoke and dust filled the sky for days until falling ash and dirt choked the San Pedro River and the fish floated belly up.

Also along the San Pedro River, the Apaches had just cornered their prized white stallion when the earthquake struck. As the soil rippled beneath their feet, the Apache warriors fell to their knees. The white stallion reared up on his hind legs. At just that moment a series of geysers erupted along the river, throwing plumes of sand and hot water 50 and 60 feet into the air.

Suddenly a giant fissure wrenched the earth. The white horse fell into the gaping crack, the chasm closed, and the horse was lost.

The 1887 Earthquake

Because of all the smoke and dust in the air, the people of Tucson could not see the Santa Catalina Mountains for four days. A prominent feature of the mountains, a peak called The Old Castle, crumbled and disappeared. Boulders came crashing down the mountain slopes.

As rocks careened through the timber, the calamity was made even worse by the sparks of forest fires. Huge plumes of smoke and dust were funneled up every canyon to hover in a huge cloud above Mount Lemmon. The next day the headlines of the *Tucson Citizen* newspaper proclaimed, *"Santa Catalina Volcano Explodes."*

Many southern Arizona residents mistook the earthquake for a volcanic eruption. All the mountain ranges in a line, the Catalinas, Huachucas, Whetstones, Dragoons, Mules, and Chiricuhuas, all burst into flames as underground gases escaped and were sparked by avalanches. Some springs flooded and others dried up. Geysers of water burst into the air in many places.

In the town of Bavispe, Mexico, the river erupted with hundreds of geysers, accompanied by tongues of fire which set the countryside ablaze. Eyewitnesses claimed the river both boiled and flooded at the same time.

When the subterranean roar preceding the earthquake had echoed throughout the hills, a mad stampede of frightened people had rushed into the mission church. Forty-eight people would die this day and 56 more were wounded, most of them when the walls of the church collapsed. It would take the rescue teams nine days to cover 40 miles, over ground rent with chasms and fissures, before they could render aid to the victims.

The legend is a bit more colorful. Folklore stories state that when the frightened citizens of Bavispe ran inside the church, every resident of Bavispe except three sought sanctuary. In the legend, when the church walls crumble everyone inside is killed. The only survivors are the harlot, the town drunk, and the mean, skeptical man of science.

The skeptical man stood atop a hill, overlooking the devastation and chortled with glee at his good luck. Never once did he express sorrow for the death of his fellow townsmen. Aghast at his lack of emotion, the town harlot ran off with the drunk and there was no one left to repopulate the town of Bavispe. It crumbled into ruin, a victim of the 1887 earthquake.

chapter 9:
The Santa Cruz Sandtrout

Every year, when the thermometer breaks 100 degrees for the first time, it is a day that Tucsonans refer to as "the day the ice breaks on the Santa Cruz River." It is a joke which not only plays on Arizona's high summer temperatures but also on the dry sandy stretches of arroyo which frequently are so-called rivers.

Another Tucson tradition also starts with the first 100-degree day of summer: the beginning of sandtrout spawning season. The sandtrout can be spotted in any of the dry washes of southern Arizona. Said to be related to the mythical Nebraska Sandcatfish the Santa Cruz Sandtrout has made amazing adaptations to the arid desert. The legendary sandtrout has been said to school beneath the sand, possessing long slender stalks which shoot up from the head and rise above the ground with eyes at the end – like periscopes.

They escape the summer heat by burrowing deep beneath the sand and only rise to the surface to spawn, eat, and breathe – breaching the desert floor like a whale, gasping for breath. It has even been said that they have blowholes.

When I was a lad, I was introduced to the legend of the Santa Cruz Sandtrout when one of the Tucson newspapers ran an article on the Outdoors page. They forgot to mention the mythical and legendary part. The story ran on April Fools' Day. So many people crowded the arroyo bridges, armed with binoculars, searching for sandtrout, that they became a traffic hazard and the newspaper was forced to confess their little joke.

During the 1970s local politicians joked about resurrecting the sandtrout. Their request for environmental-riparian-protection funds had been denied for the Santa Cruz River because of a Washington mandate that only rivers with fish qualified as riparian zones.

I was delighted in the 1980s to see my old high school science teacher, Mr. Torgeson, win a local "columnist for a day" contest with a story he wrote detailing the habits of the Santa Cruz Sandtrout. Once again, over the next several days people were standing on bridges, searching for glimpses of the elusive dry-land fish. Indeed, many such sightings were reported.

So now I hope to inspire other people to look for the Santa Cruz Sandtrout. Many of my best memories as a young man are my recollections of lazy summer days spent sandtrout fishing.

The only known natural predator of the Santa Cruz Sandtrout is the fisherman. To fish one of Arizona's sandy arroyos you first need the proper boat; something with four wheel drive, and the tires jacked up so high that the feeling while riding inside is like you are continuously pole vaulting. In Tucson we refer to such a vehicle as a galleon in the Rillito River Armada.

Horned toad, favorite bait of the sandtrout

The typical crew of a Rillito River Armada galleon consists of a captain, a navigator, and a dog. Any experienced desert angler can tell you that the best bait for sandtrout is the horned toad.

The horned toad is a prehistoric-looking little reptile whose armored head makes him look like a dinosaur. Here is another cool, barbaric fact – horned toads can spit blood out their eyes. If you want to catch sandtrout, you first have to capture a horned toad.

Snagging one of the little reptilian ant eaters as they scurry across the hot desert sand is not as easy as it sounds. Horned toads are protected animals but there is nothing in any government regulations that says you cannot put a leash around his barbed, armored head and take him for a walk.

Once you have captured your bait you have to pick a suitable spot in the arroyo and creep up on the elusive sandtrout from the bank above. The Arizona angler ties his horned toad to the line and casts him over a palo verde or mesquite tree, sending the horned toad flying through the air. As soon as his claws hit sand, the horned toad begins to scurry atop the arroyo floor.

Soon eyestalks rise above the sand, periscope style, as the sandtrout eyes its prey. The sandtrout swims forward, eyestalks cutting ripples through the loose soil, tiny plume of dust rising behind like a wake. A large bull sandtrout will frequently leap all the way out of the sand as it lunges for its prey, swallowing the unfortunate reptile in a single gulp. That is when the barbed head of the sand trout sets itself like a hook.

Hungry fisherman reel in the sandtrout as fast as they can. On a hot, summer day, when the sun has heated the sand to 100 and teens, a fish reeled in fast enough will cook itself from all the friction.

For those with a more laid back fishing style there is a

traditional recipe below:

Sonoran Style Sandtrout:
    17 parts tequila
    2 parts lime
    1 part chili peppers

Mix the ingredients together into a marinade. Take fish. Throw fish to the dog. Captain and navigator drink marinade all night long.

Oh yeah, one more tip about Santa Cruz sandtrout fishing. If your local arroyo has been experiencing heavy monsoons – the type that cause flash floods – then don't even bothering looking for sandtrout. When one of our normally dry washes has an unexpected bank to bank flow, all the fish drown.

Arizona sandtrout

chapter 10:
Thunder Mountain

Old Pop Corn still draws the Patagonia Mountains during deer-hunting season but today we search for copper deposits. The forest is thick with signs of game; big buck antelope, doe deer with yearling, bear feces and wild turkey. The Boone and Crockett world-record jaguar was bagged in these rugged hills.

We ascend and descend the steep slopes, machetes hacking a path through thick brush, scrub oak, manzanita, and chircuahua pine. We sweat, curse, moan, bleed, and groan while butterflies flutter effortlessly by. The sara orangetip and purplevine swallowtail float like bobbing flowers. We pause to rest on the crest of a ridgetop. I survey the mountains on the horizon, the crowns of the Patagonias, American Peak, Red Mountain, and the collapsed cavernous crater of Thunder Mountain, the red and crimson volcanic heart of the Patagonia range.

This day our journey of geology takes us past the deserted ghost towns of Harshaw, Washington Camp, Mowry, and Lochiel. They are old mining camps that went boom and bust, and then went completely under when prohibition was repealed and the passageways were emptied of smugglers and bootleggers.

Pop Corn tells me that these rugged piles of earth, mountains we will traverse for days, once fell from the sky. Although these mountains are volcanic, there is no caldera here. These mountains were shot through the air by an unknown cinder cone like a sneeze of fiery phlegm, a red hot magma raindrop scorching the heavens, a rain of molten lava which landed in this spot with a plop.

These instant mountains have an ancient history dating

back to conquistador silver mines in 1637. The names of the ranches in this region still reflect the legacy of Spanish land grants. They are haciendas like San Antonio and Santo Nino. We seek shade in the doorway of the only remaining wall of an adobe ruin, lunching near the terraced hills of the Harshaw graveyard, viewing tombstones brightly adorned with plastic flowers.

Pop Corn tells me that 35 years ago his first geology crew found an old muzzle loader rifle in these hills. It was probably lost by an old Spanish prospector during his battles with *manzanita*, bear, and jaguar. That blunderbuss must have roared like a dinosaur, with booming echoes banging off volcanic rocks, bouncing off the walls of Thunder Mountain.

Even the roar of the mighty blunderbuss is temporary, lost for centuries under a *manzanita* bush, fading into silence and bird calls, just like the people in the graves at Harshaw. Those old bones are drowning under a sea of plastic flowers that once represented the laughter of children.

We finish lunch and walk onwards, all day, day after day, until our work here is done. Today we stroll along the abandoned road to the Big Chief Mine, struggling with obstacles of thorn, angle, and geometry. I am grateful for my opportunity to add my echoes to the Thunder Mountain dome, my pockets full of peacock ore.

chapter 11:
Local Place Names

Look at a map, any map, and the names of the places will make the words unfold like stories. The diversity of names on a map reveal the diversity of cultures which have lived here. Every name carries the stamp of a different people, reflecting a wide rainbow of legend, history, and fable.

As you would suspect, many of the regional names originate with the oldest peoples to live here; the Native American cultures. No group of people lived here longer than the O'odham, descendants of the Hohokam and beyond.

The city of Tucson is derived from the O'odham word *Chukson*. *Chukson* is a word which translates loosely as "black base," a reference to the color of Sentinel Peak (sometimes referred to as A Mountain) where the ancient Native Americans farmed along the Santa Cruz River.

Other colorful O'odham names include *Pan Tak* (Coyote Sitting) and *Pisenemo* (Bison Head). The first Arizona mountains named on a map were named with O'odham words. The Huachuca Mountains were described in 1690, sketched in by the hand of Juan Mateo Manje, military consort to Father Kino. *Huachuca* is said to have been the name of a small O'odham rancheria in the area.

The Whetstone Mountains are currently named after a fine-grained rock that was once mined here to sharpen cutlery. The name Whetstone did not appear on a map until 1859 when they were described repeatedly by Colonel B. L. E. Bonneville. Spanish maps locate the same mountains as early as the 1780s and named the range the Sierra del Babocamari.

Although the Opata name for the mountain has

Sculpture of Sedona Schnebly whom the town of Sedona is named after

disappeared, the language stills endures in the name of Babocamari Creek. Like the ghosts of the Opata, many Arizona old-time cowboys like to recall the early decades of the 20th century when there was still water in the Babocamarai and a man could drop a fishing line with high expectations. The *Chiricahua Mountains* are named after Opata words believed to mean "mountain of the wild turkeys."

The Chiricahua Apache were named by the Opata word for the mountains they lived in. The Apache words for the mountain where they lived was *tsil kawa* or "great mountain." Apache names dot the landscape. Beautiful Aravaipa Canyon is derived from the name of the Apache tribe who lived there. The Aravaipa Apache were led by a chief called *Eskinmizin* and their name meant "People of the Dark Rock."

Pinal County's name was derived from Apache words. Emory named mountains on both sides of the Gila River the *Pino Lanos* Mountains, believed to be the name of the local Apache tribe. On later maps, the name was changed to the *Pinalenos*, but Emory's name for the highest peak in southeastern Arizona, Mt. Graham, remained.

While some of the old Spanish place names have been replaced or usurped, many still remain. I have a theory that many of the Spanish explorers must have been hungry. There are names such as the *Pelconcillo Mountains* (Sugar Loaf), *Pan Quemado* (Burnt Bread), and the towns of *Ajo* (Garlic) and *Calabazes* (Pumpkin).

Sometimes Spanish names were descriptive such as *Dos Cabezas*, which means "two heads" referring to two bald peaks. Sometimes the names were redundant such as taking the Spanish word for peak (*picacho*) and the word for little river (*rillito*) to come up with Picacho Peak and Rillito River.

There were many map-making wandering missionaries and their names always included saints such as the Santa Rosa, Santa Rita, or Santa Catalina Mountains. In 1775, Father Garces must have been feeling particularly mystical when he named the mountains east of Phoenix the *Estrella* or "star mountains."

Sometimes a place can bear many different names all at once. For instance, the Santa Catalina Mountains still carry the name given to them by Father Kino in the 1690s. Father Kino was visiting an Apache missionary *"visita"* at a place he gave the longer title of *Santa Catalina de Cuitabagu*. *De Cuitabagu* are Apache words referring to "a spring where mesquite beans grow." The ancient name for these same mountains is given to them by the O'odham who called the range *Babad Duag* or the "Frog Mountains," after the tiny gray amphibians who live amidst the waterfalls and granite pools, blending in perfect camouflage with the colors of the rocks. Many people today refer only to the highest peak and call the whole entire range Mt. Lemmon.

Mount Lemmon is named after a woman, Sarah Jane Plummer, who wed scientist John Lemmon. The two of them arrived in Arizona on a "botanical wedding trip" hoping to name some new species in the name of exploration. As the newlyweds and their guide began what they thought was the first ascent of the mountain, the excited husband stopped suddenly at what is now called Dan's Saddle.

Lemmon grabbed a pine tree branch and shouted, "All hats off!"

He had just discovered a new plant species, the "*Pinus Arizonica.*" Once they reached the top of the highest peak, believing they were the first to climb the mountain, their guide carved their initials into a tall tree to signify their feat. They soon found burro tracks which led to a small hunter's cabin. The two half-starved trappers said there had been others on top of the mountain before them as well.

Sarah Lemmon was still believed to be the first woman to climb the mountain and the peak is named after her. It is possible that Mount Lemmon is the only mountain in the world named after a female explorer. East of Wilcox are the Mae West Peaks but they may wear that name for a different reason.

The Americans were the most recent arrivals, but they did not hesitate to start naming places. Peppersauce Wash and hence Peppersauce Cave is named after a hungry prospector who lost a bottle of peppersauce there after pausing to eat. The Empire Mountains are named after the Empire Ranch, founded in 1876 by Walter Vail.

Some places are named after soldiers such as the Dragoon Mountains, where the 3rd U.S. Cavalry, known as the Dragoons were stationed. The town of Kearny is named after General Phillip Kearny who led explorations down the Gila River in the war with Mexico. The original Camp Lowell, later to be known as Fort Lowell, was founded by Colonel West and the California Volunteers. Camp Lowell was established during the Civil War when the California Volunteers were chasing a Confederate column. The camp was named after Brigadier General Lowell who had only recently become a battle casualty.

Settlers led by Levi Ruggles arrived to farm the Gila River Valley in 1868. By 1870 there were so many settlers that it was decided that the new community needed a name. Given the honor, Territorial Governor McCormack named the new town *Florence*, after his sister. Named recently (in 1926), the town of *Coolidge* was named after the building of the Coolidge Dam that made farming profitable enough for a small community to arise. An even more recent name is the tragic *Tom Mix Wash*, named after the popular cowboy movie star who died in an automobile wreck there.

Probably my favorite story among Arizona place names is the one author Edwin Corle tells in his history of the Gila River. In his book *The Gila*, Corle gives a version of how Phoenix received its name. On October 20, 1870, a meeting was called to give definition to the loose collection of settlers that was beginning to crop up. A set of boundaries was decided upon and all that remained for the assembly to decide was a name.

There were many suggestions. One man, a sympathizer of the fallen Confederacy, offered to call the city *Stonewall* in honor of rebel general Stonewall Jackson. Since these early citizens were hoping for federal aid, honoring a rebel leader did not seem to be a good idea. Another suggested *Salina* after the Salt River which the Spaniards had named *Rio Salina*.

It is at this point that a roguish character in Phoenix history appears. He was known as Lord Duppa but, except for his English accent, he never offered any proof of his royal heritage. Duppa quickly downed a couple of drinks. The strong spirits gave him courage and he stepped up to the podium. He made a wonderful speech which even used a smattering of Greek and Latin words to dazzle the crowd.

Duppa's speech was filled with wondrous descriptions of the canals and ruins of the vanished Hohokam civilization.

"A great race once dwelt here," he stated, "and another great race will dwell here in the future. I prophesy that a new city will arise Phoenix-like from the ashes and ruins of the old."

It was at this point that the intoxicated speaker tumbled from the podium.

Still, the audience was impressed by these eloquent words and stood to applaud the fallen speaker. The town is still known to this day as Phoenix, but legends hold that, after Duppa was hoisted and carried away, it was discovered he had left a whiskey bottle under the podium, a brand of whiskey whose label read *"Phoenix."*

chapter 12:
Papago Dictionary

Searching a used book store, digging through western history, geology, gunfighters and soiled doves, I discovered an unexpected treasure; a *Papago / English Dictionary*. It had been compiled by Lucille and Dean Sexton in 1969 for the University of Arizona Press. It was the largest, most-comprehensive dictionary of the native language ever compiled at the time.

Even the title dates the book; the name *Papago* is no longer politically correct for this nation of Native Americans. The name Papago came from a translation misunderstanding.

When explorers marched from Mexico City to the northern frontier of New Spain, they came upon natives who farmed the desert. When the Spanish asked, through their guides, what these people called themselves the question was misinterpreted as "What are you eating?" The good natured people replied, "We are eating beans," which in their language sounded roughly like Papago. Thus they became the bean eaters for the next few centuries.

In the last decades of the 20th century, casino money began to roll into the reservation. One of the first things the tribal government did with the money was run a public-relations campaign to change their name. They are now known by the name they call themselves, the *Tohono O'odham* or "Desert People."

After I acquired the dictionary I could not wait to get home and read the language, learn the way the words fit the land and described the birds and animals. I was eager to discover the word for saguaro because the O'odham claim that saguaros are people too.

First, I explored one of the appendixes in the back, a map

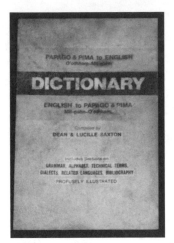

Papago Dictionary compiled by Dean and Lucille Sexton

with all the places using their O'odham names and translations. Any wizard, brujo or shaman, will tell you that place names are filled with history and magic. The most magical place on the reservation is *Baboquivari Peak* (mountain that is fat in the middle), home to Elder Brother Iiyotoi.

Next to Baboquivari is a town known to the O'odham as *Gogs Mek* or Burnt Dog. The town of *Sells* is named for an early trader but the local name translates as Turtle Wedged. *Pisenimo* is derived from the words *Pisin Mo'o* which mean Bison Skull.

Tucson is the Spanish translation of *Chukson* which means spring at the base of a black hill, a reference to the farms at the base of what is now A Mountain. There is still a town on the reservation called *Ali Chukson* or "Little Tucson."

The giant, green saguaro, the harvest of whose sugary red fruit signaled the new year, is called *hashani*. The honey mesquite tree or *kui* has beans, which like saguaro fruit can be turned into wine. Some plants sound like their names such as *ho'idkam* for the gnarled ironwood trees or *ahn* to describe the soft lavender flowers of the desert willow.

My favorite cactus fruit comes from a tiny thorny cactus which grows in the shade of large stones on steep slopes. This pin-cushion cactus known as *bahban haishwig* has small football-shaped red fruits that taste like a cross between a tomato and a raspberry.

The large raptor that you see flying in the sky or perched atop a telephone pole is probably a *huapal* or red-tailed hawk.

The word for javelina, *kohji*, almost sounds Japanese. The jackrabbit is *chuhwi* and the bighorn sheep goes by *cheshoni*. Coyote and all his trickster brothers call themselves *ban*. If you see a *muhwal* better kill it quick because, according to O'odham tradition, flies are messengers of death.

OhshaD is the name for the jaguar and that fact reminds me that jaguars used to be common here.

The butterflies which flutter by the flowers are known as *hohokimal*. When my friend and I discovered a narrow canyon in the Tortolita Mountains where one of the boulders held a beautiful butterfly petroglyph we named it Hohokimal Canyon.

This butterfly is a large petroglyph with perfect spirals as wings. One spiral twists one way and the other spins in the opposite direction. This adds mystery to meaning.

The spiral maze is an important symbol in O'odham mythology. The maze with the man in the middle is an ubiquitous O'odham symbol and has many layers of meaning. It can represent one's journey through life, the path to sanctuary, or the road to enlightenment. Spirals in Chaco Canyon and the Tucson Mountains were used to measure astronomical events. Petroglyph spirals have been said to give directions such as upstream and downstream.

I can remember standing in that narrow canyon, staring at the spiral wings of that beautiful butterfly petroglyph, awed by the mystery. I suddenly realized that learning the secrets of the language of the land is going to take a lifetime.

Monument to Navajo Code Talkers, downtown Phoenix

chapter 13:
Piesetewa Peak

(pronounced *pi-s-to-wah*)

When a daring military operation rescued Jessica Lynch from the Iraqi hospital where she was being held as prisoner of war, an entire nation beamed with pride. The rescue team also brought back with them remains of eleven American soldiers who had perished in battle. Among the fallen was Lori Piesetewa, a 23-year-old single mother who was a member of the Hopi Nation and lived in Tuba City, Arizona on the Navajo Reservation. Piesetewa is believed to be the first female Native American soldier to be killed in combat while serving in the U.S. military.

The tradition of Native American women aiding our armed forces goes back to the Revolutionary War. At the Battle of Oriskany, an Oneida woman named Tyonajanegen fought on horseback at her husband's side. Tyonajanegen rushed into the fray when she saw her husband get shot in the wrist. The valiant married couple rode and fought side by side, Tyonajanegen loading her wounded husband's rifle so he might shoot again and again.

Sacagewa is probably the most famous woman to serve our military, acting as guide and interpreter for the Lewis and Clark expedition. Sacagewa joined the expedition only because she was the teenage bride of a French trapper named Touissant Charbonneau.

Soon, Lewis and Clark's regard of the French trapper dropped considerably and their opinion of Sacagewa rose steeply. Historians like to joke that Sacagewa did everything Lewis and Clark did, but with a child strapped to her back. The young woman's ability to forage for wild artichokes, licorice, and prairie turnips kept the soldiers alive many times. She was responsible for one vegetable appearing in your local grocery store.

The root salsify, was one of Captain Merriweather's favorite dishes. Salsify looks like a dirty, furry carrot but, when you peel off the outer skin, it reveals a white vegetable. Captain Lewis liked his salsify sautéed over the campfire with a little butter and green onions.

Sacagawea was kidnapped as a child and raised by another tribe. While translating for Lewis and Clark, she was unexpectedly reunited with her long-lost brother, now a Shoshone chief. This led to honored treatment for the expedition. Upon their return to St. Louis, Sacagewa was presented with a commission in the military.

The last battle of the Civil War took place between two different Native American forces from the same tribe. Stand Watie rode his two companies of Cherokee Mounted Rifles past Union lines to burn down the Cherokee capital in the Oklahoma Territory. This included torching the famous Rose Cottage of his Cherokee rival, John Ross. Stand Watie, known to his people as *Degataga* or "immovable", was the last Confederate general to surrender, laying down his sword on June 23, 1865.

Four Native American Catholic nuns from South Dakota served in the Spanish American War, working as nurses. By World War I the number of Native Americans women serving the military as nurses had expanded to more than 800.

Matthew Juan, a member of the Pima nation, was the first Native American soldier to die in World War I. The Pima continued their proud record of service to our nation in World War II with Ira Hayes. Ira Hayes was among the soldiers photographed raising the flag on Iwo Jima. This well published picture became one of the most heroic icons of the war.

When World War II broke out there were no dictionaries of the Navajo language. The Navajo Codetalkers served in the Pacific theaters of action and spoke to each other in their native language. A recent movie starring Nicolas Cage, titled

Windtalkers recently commemorated the experience.

My favorite story was recorded by the journalist Ernie Pyle who described how the Navajo soldiers prepared themselves for the invasion of Okinawa, staining their faces with paint and improvising ceremonial dress with chicken feathers, seashells, coconut, and spent rifle cartridges. Pyle observed several thousand grim-faced Marines watching as the Navajos danced and chanted before the battle. The Navajos even translated the *Marine Corps Hymn* into their native language.

After the ceremony, as the convoy was headed into battle, Pyle asked a Navajo private if he felt that the ceremony had worked. The young man pointed to a rainbow hovering above the ships.

Cozy Stanley Brown, who served as a Codetalker, described taking a Japanese scalp in one of the fierce battles for the tiny islands of the Pacific. Brown brought the scalp all the way back to his Arizona home so that a medicine man named Stewart Grayeyes could perform a purifying ritual.

An Apache shaman named Willie Neal saw his reputation grow immensely. He taught seven Apache recruits the secrets of bat magic so that they might bob, flutter, and weave to dodge bullets. All seven soldiers returned from World War II.

The day after the tragic events of 9/11 a newspaper on the Sioux reservation proclaimed, "An attack on America is an attack on Indian land!" Today both our northern and southern borders are defended by special units of Native Americans. In the Arctic, a special unit of the National Guard known as the Eskimo Scouts includes 60 Native American women. In the arid deserts along the Arizona/ Mexico border a special band of Native American trackers known as Shadow Wolves search the rugged arroyos and canyons for drug smugglers and potential terrorists on behalf of the Border Patrol.

Lori Piesetewa continued the proud tradition of Native American service and sacrifice for this nation when she became the first Native American woman to die in combat. Just as the roles of Native Americans and women have expanded in the military, so has the risk. Lori was serving as a mechanic and leaves behind two small sons.

Former Arizona governor Janet Napolitano, wants to change the name of one of Phoenix's more prominent landmarks to Lori Piesetewa Peak. The motion has been clouded in controversy because of a law which states that a person must be dead for at least five years before a geographical feature can be named after them. Some people claim the governor has used strong-arm tactics to push the measure through. Interestingly, no one has come to the defense of the old name which was Squaw Peak. The word *squaw* is based upon slang used by French trappers for the private parts of a Native American woman. Most Native Americans find the term highly offensive.

Much of the controversy about renaming Piesetewa Peak has centered on the timing and the five-year rule. Native American support for the name change has been vocal. A resident of the San Carlos Apache Reservation, Loren Victor, spoke at a recent hearing: "Native American people have been the recipients of many broken treaties over the years. Let's break one more and rename that thing today."

At the funeral service for Piesetewa, a retired Army chaplain, a Hopi, and a friend of the Piesetewa family, Caleb Johnson, reminded listeners of the Hopi tradition which states that when a Hopi dies his spirit returns to the earth as a blessing of moisture for the parched desert earth. On the day the military aircraft carrying Lori Piesetewa's remains touched down on American soil in Washington DC it snowed on the Hopi Reservation. It was on a day unusually late in the year for snowfall in the Painted Desert. The late snow moistened the earth and ensured that there would be plenty of spring flowers blooming for Easter.

Welcome home, Lori.

chapter 14:
Japanese Relocation Camps

During World War II, President Franklin Roosevelt signed Executive Order 9066, known as The Relocation and Enemies Act. Over 100,000 Americans of Japanese descent and their immigrant parents were rounded up and confined in relocation centers. This included nearly the entire Japanese-American population of the Pacific Coast.

In Arizona there were three relocation centers; Poston, Gila River and Luepp.

With more than 18,000 residents, Poston was the third largest population center in Arizona in 1942. Mary Masunaga was interviewed more than three decades later and an edited version of this interview is included in the book Arizona Memories.

Mrs. Masunaga was shipped from coastal California to the Arizona desert as a young bride. Seven-and-a-half months pregnant, she left for Poston on April 15, 1942, with two suitcases, all she was allowed to carry. Her daughter was born on the first of July, on a day when the temperature reached 124 degrees. The proud mother named her daughter after the month of her birth, July Masunaga.

Masunaga described how dehumanizing it felt to be unloaded from the train and forced to wear large brown pieces of paper with identification numbers. Then they were fingerprinted. All of the families gathered there faced different degrees of financial ruin. The men in the camps did a lot of pacing, looking for something productive to do, worrying about how to rebuild their family futures when and if they were ever released.

Mrs. Masunaga said the worst memory for her was, "the lack of privacy because I was recently married and having to be in one room with a bachelor and my mother in law . . . It was the most torturous kind of experience." Mrs. Masunaga gave birth to three children in the relocation camps.

The Gila River Internment Center consisted of two camps, totaling more than 13,000 people. Both Canal Camp and Butte Camp were located on the Gila River Indian Reservation. The internees began to arrive at Butte Camp on August 21, 1942. By March 21, 1943, Butte Camp had reached a peak population of 8,301. There were five churches in the camp, both Buddhist and Christian denominations. The citizens of Butte Camp published a newspaper called the *Gila News Courier*, with columns in both Japanese and English. The enterprising Japanese Americans even scavenged materials to build a baseball field, getting credit for introducing the game of baseball to the Pima Indians.

The Gila River Indian Community gave permission for a memorial to be erected not far from Sacaton in honor of the Japanese-American experience on reservation land. The monument was built at the site of Butte Camp, atop a small hill overlooking the camp. Many of the concrete building foundations are still there, small rectangles in orderly rows.

The Kishiyama family was detained in Butte Camp. They sat in the back of a military truck with other Japanese Americans, heading towards someplace they had never seen, clouds of dust rising behind them. The Kishiyamas sat on crowded benches, holding hands. Their thoughts were far from the Arizona desert.

Their only child, their son George, was back in Japan. The Kishiyamas had been afraid that young George was growing up without an awareness of his cultural heritage and sent him back to Japan for his education. When the Japanese military struck Pearl Harbor, George was separated from his family by the vastness of the Pacific Ocean.

During the war, George was forced to report to the Tokyo police station every day. He said that schoolmates, teachers, and even relatives would whisper or stop talking when he walked into the room. George did not know which side was winning the war until the bombs began to fall on Tokyo.

Once they started, the bombs fell day and night; fire, death, and destruction raining down on Tokyo. Everyone prayed to stay alive, George recalled that the bombs were as likely to kill an American citizen like him as anyone else. When the war ended, George Kishiyama returned home to the United States. He was stunned to learn that, while he was gone, his parents had been forced to sell everything they owned and they were imprisoned in Arizona.

After the war, the Kishiyamas remained in Arizona, starting a small flower farm. I remember as a child, driving along Baseline Road, on the outskirts of Phoenix, and gazing in awe at the rows and rows of flowers farms; the dazzling fields of colors. Many Japanese Americans were nestled among the flower farmers, transcending the ordeal of the internment camps. Now, as Phoenix grows into an ever larger metropolis; the flower farms are being swallowed up by urban developments.

Despite being placed in internment camps, all Japanese males of the appropriate age were expected to fulfill their military obligations. Many Japanese Americans volunteered to serve in the military. These men saw battle in the Pacific and European fronts and conducted themselves with honor. A small handful of men refused service. Some of these men protested all wars for spiritual reasons and others protested for constitutional reasons; stating that they would not fight to defend a country that had imprisoned their family. These men faced estrangement from their own community for their stand.

The conscientious objectors were placed on the steep and

rocky slopes of the Santa Catalinas. They went to Sycamore Prison Camp, where they worked alongside other prisoners, building the Hitchcock Highway up Mount Lemmon.

Little remains of Sycamore Prison Camp except concrete foundations, the dam and reservoir, plus a handful of peach trees planted by the prisoners; trees which still bear ripe fruit. In August of 2003, the Forest Service erected a monument honoring the contributions of these citizens. Many of these imprisoned conscientious objectors, most of them Buddhist monks, returned for the ceremony.

At Butte Camp, on the reservation, not far from the Gila River where the relocation camp once stood, there is a much older monument. This monument stands atop a hill. It is a piece of simple architecture, soft curves somehow making a sad and poignant statement. The structure almost looks like a series of big picture windows – perhaps giving us a chance to stare into our national soul.

The Butte Camp monument was originally dedicated on April 23, 1944, while the camp was still open. I close my eyes and try imagine the scene; a crowd of small Oriental faces listening to speeches as the flag waved in the breeze. The memorial was built to honor those Japanese Americans who served as soldiers in World War II. In many of these camps, the young Japanese Americans who served as soldiers were revered as heroes in these small, tight-knit communities. A list of the men includes traditional Japanese names such as Tatsumi Furukawa and Takanori Nishi, plus names that revealed assimilation, such as John Hashimoto or George Masumoto.

The sun slowly sets, the shadows of the memorial fading into the dusk. Sunset feels like the appropriate time to be at a war memorial, and I offer a moment of silence and reflection before moving on my way.

chapter 15:
Frog Mountain Pools

Only one of the Tohono O'odham names for local mountain ranges still appears on the maps. The Tucson Mountains retained their indigenous name. *Santa Rita, Rincon*, and *Santa Catalina* were the names given to these ranges by their Spanish explorers. *Mt. Wrightston*, the highest of the peaks in the area, was known to the O'odham as "the long one." The Rincons were called "the turkey necks" and were supposed to be a stronghold of feminine magic. The Santa Catalinas were referred to as *Babad Duag* or "Frog Mountains."

Being known as The Frog Mountains was quite an honor. Frogs were sacred to desert farming peoples such as the O'odham. Their summer monsoon ceremonies would include toasts with saguaro wine and songs of praise to the croaking amphibians. Why would a desert peoples revere frogs? Probably because of the frogs' association with water and rain.

A resident of the Frog Mountain Pools

The hottest month of the summer was known to the O'odham as "the painful moon." To survive, the tribe would break into smaller family units who would creep up into the mountains where there was water which did not dry up even during the worst months of summer. The Santa Catalina Mountains hold many geological folds and granite canyons, which contain an ideal habitat for the little gray frogs that thrive in monsoon fed pools.

The same liquid pools that provide a playground for frogs

can do the same for humans. The streams which catapult over boulders provide an oasis sanctuary to escape the summer heat. The frog pools of the Catalinas attract many visitors every year to places such as Sabino Canyon, Catalina State Park, and Buehman Canyon.

My favorite of the Frog Mountain Pools is the steep chain of waterfalls called the "Cataracts." There is no official trail head and the recent highway construction has made a rugged hike even tougher. For those willing to brave this rugged adventure here is how you get there.

Take the Catalina Highway past the old prison camp and watch for the nine-mile marker. The road will wind back and forth with cliffs on one side of the road and nothing except a guard rail on the other. Just before the 10-mile marker, just before the road enters Upper Bear Canyon, the string of guard rails is interrupted by a small parking lot next to a rather undistinguished dirt hill. There is little earth on this side of the highway but a lot of slope and a gaping chasm

I love that chasm – it weeds out the tourists and leaves the Cataracts a relatively secluded place. That chasm represents the steepness of the slope which makes this stretch the most frequently washed out part of the Hitchcock Highway. This chasm is a result of the dramatic geological pressures which formed the steep, winding waterfalls of the Cataracts.

From the parking lot, one can see the granite structure of the mountain bending at sharp angles. By peering carefully, some of the pools and waterfalls are barely visible from the road.

The steepness of the slope prevents the establishment of a well-maintained trail, but there are faint traces of foot paths made by previous travelers. Hike along the base of the hill before descending down the highly eroded rockslide to the stream. The terrain is steep and rocky but it is a deceptively short distance to the first stream. This is not the same stream which feeds the waterfalls and pools that are visible from the road. Following this stream does lead to some gorgeous winding passages of smoothed granite where the stream hangs a sudden, sharp, right-angle turn and culminates in a tall, twisting waterfall but these are not the Cataracts.

To get to the main falls, it is best to back track to where you first approach the stream and cross it, circling above the main pools and dropping down to them. There is no official trail but there are several well-worn footpaths on the other side of the stream. They traverse the rolling ridge at a consistent elevation. These paths crisscross and all generally lead to a spectacular overlook in about the middle of the waterfall chain. Once you reach this spot, either direction, up or downstream will lead to waterfalls and crystal-clear pools.

I would advise going upstream in search of *The Old Man*. I have never been certain whether the name, Old Man, referred to the large tree whose lightning scarred carcass can be seen from the road or if the name referred to the deep, dark, reflective pool beside it. This seemingly bottomless pool is not only fed by the stream which drops into it from the precipice above, but also water from the cliffs which tower above it. The earth works as a sieve as the water flows beneath the soil. This pool always has enough water for a cool refreshing swim no matter how severe the summer drought. Be forewarned that, no matter how warm the day, the water is always bone-chilling cold.

There are large waterfalls leading into and dropping away from this particular pool, but the waterfall leading into The Old Man is flat-out gorgeous. The current descends over about 140 feet of well-polished granite, performing a spiral as graceful as an ice skater's pirouette, before dropping into the bottomless pool with a splash. The Old Man is one of my favorite spots on this earth. I included it in a piece of fiction. The following excerpt is from my story, *The Gadsden Arizona Revolt*.

"Sitting next to the pool known as The Old Man, Damon watched the swallows barrel roll as they soared by, dipping low enough to make the water ripple as they passed. When the ripples stilled, Damon saw in the water's reflection a gathering of people, Tadpole amongst them. Drums beat and gradually voices rose in chanting songs. There were the songs of frogs, songs praising the earth, songs about songs, and anthems welcoming the rain and harvest.

Seven Cataracts

"Slowly at first, the men began to dance in a circle. Their feet shuffled across the earth, stirring up dirt as their voices rang out with the song of frogs. Tadpole sang loudly until his voice was hoarse. Pausing, Tadpole cleansed his throat with saguaro fruit wine. It seemed the saguaros listened. Their green trunks vibrated with the resonance of celebratory voices, lifting the chanted words skyward with their uplifted arms."

I hope you enjoy your adventure and journey at the Cataracts. Remember to be careful. Remember to watch closely. Do not be surprised if you do not see the magic beings until they jump. The granite geology which forms the Cataracts also provides a home to countless tiny, gray frogs whose camouflage blends in indistinguishably with the stone. When the frogs hop they are much easier to spot; suddenly flying a short distance through the air. It is almost as if the mountain itself is spawning frogs.

chapter 16:
Ironwood Tree National Monument

Bruce Babbitt visited southern Arizona while he was still Secretary of the Interior and made an unexpected proposal. Scrambling up the steep, rocky slopes of Ragged Top Peak, Babbitt asked one of his aides to pull some strands of barbed wire apart so the Secretary could slip past a fence. The native Arizonan turned and faced the desert landscape spreading across the horizon. Babbitt was about to suggest that some of this scenic beauty be preserved forever in the form of an Ironwood Tree National Monument.

President Clinton put pen to the paper and put Ironwood Tree National Monument into law. Inside the boundaries are 114,000 acres including Ragged Top and much of the Silverbell Mountains as well as a part of the Waterman-Roskruge Mountains. Small pockets of wilderness in the Tortolita Mountains and Pinal County have been included within the monument boundaries in an attempt to save the habitat of the endangered ferreguinous pygmy owl.

The Rockland Hotel at Ironwood Tree National Monument

Private landowners in the Ragged Top area managed to convince the government to include sections west of the Silverbell Mountains and the Samaneigo Hills to protect the only large herd of bighorn sheep in the Tucson vicinity. The area already holds large water tanks erected by sportsmen. The tanks are known as guzzlers, put in place for large game animals such as deer and bighorn sheep.

The diversity of flora and fauna in the area is considered to be one of the strongest reasons for placing it under protected status. This region holds more than 64 species of mammals including *javelina*, bobcat, jackrabbit, and mountain lion. The skies above Ragged Top are filled with 57 varieties of birds. There are 25 species of ants that live there and more than188 types of bees.

The new national monument includes more than 250 plant species and features some of the thickest ironwood-tree forests in the world. In some sub regions of the Sonoran Desert the ironwood tree is the dominant nurse plant for such cacti as organ pipe and saguaro. Studies have shown that ironwood and other pod-bearing trees can increase the diversity of bird species in desert scrub habitat by 63 percent.

On a recent visit to the new monument in early May, the ironwood trees were in bloom. These gnarled hardwood trees wear tiny lavender flowers which hover about the crowns of the trees like delicate wreaths, shimmering in the breeze. The saguaro cacti were also blooming. The large yellow and white blossoms are not only the state flower, but harvesting the ripe red fruit of the columnar giant cacti signals the beginning of the O'odham new year.

In the late spring, the palo verde trees join the ironwood and saguaro in bloom. These small green trees become covered with bouquets of bright yellow flowers which seem to attract bees from everywhere. The O'odham have legends about *palo verde* trees, calling her spirit the "witch in the yellow dress."

In the late spring the witch in the yellow dress appears on hilltops. The yellow flowers that comprise her garment flutter in the breeze as she beckons to the curious and young at heart saying, "Come follow me, the next canyon, the next valley is even more beautiful with even more flowers."

The O'odham use this legend to explain those hikers who are so enchanted with the beauty of a desert springtime that they hike further and further, always wanting to see the beauty beckoning just over the next ridge or just beyond the next hill until they have gone too far and become lost.

This particular day I have come to explore the southern edge of the Ironwood Monument – a place called Cocoraque Butte. I take a good guess as to which dirt road will lead closest to the Butte and park the car. The flat spot where I have parked my automobile, just past the cattle gate, is also the home to a huge colony of digger bees.

There are literally thousands of tiny holes that dot the ground where the digger bees have placed their homes. It is as many bees as I can recall ever having seen at any one time. They too enjoy the wide array of flowers.

Cocoraque Butte has been placed on the National Historic Register on account of the large prehistoric village there as well as for the stupendous examples of petroglyph rock art. Many of these rock art sites are still considered sacred by both the O'odham and Hopi nations. While there are thousands of petroglyph symbols carved into the rocks here, there is also a small handful of cowboy graffiti as well. Most of the cowboy graffiti has dates in the 1920s and 30s. One looking straight up at Cocoraque Butte has a date of 1885.

The petroglyphs at Cocoraque Butte include a boulder which has a googly eyed figure almost three feet high, representative of the Aztec rain god Tlaloc.

At the northern edge of Ironwood Monument, the Silverbell Mountains hold another prehistoric village. Cerro Prieto is an example of the classical Hohokam period, dating from 700 to 1200 AD. This walled fortress on the steep slopes of the north side would have provided optimum protection from raiders and invaders. Cerro Prieto is located just inside the Pinal County line and contains more than 250 masonry rooms and many stone compounds, as well as metates, canals, and plenty of pottery. One intriguing feature of Cerro Prieto is the long stone wall near the top of the hill, known to archaeologists as trincheras. No one knows for certain whether these long stone walls were for defense or religious purposes or marked clan boundaries.

When I first became acquainted with the Silverbell Mountains it was while working with a geology crew. Every morning we would drive past the open-pit mine and crane our necks to try and catch a glimpse of the bighorn sheep that could sometimes be seen on the terraced slopes. That same year I had gone to my local used-book store and traded a stack of books by obscurely famous dead guys and picked up some new reading material, including an O'odham dictionary.

As the geology truck rolled across the landscape I would flip through my dictionary and try to imagine the sounds of the language of the land. I wondered which words the original inhabitants had used to describe the names of the towns and mountains. What did they call the plants and animals? The word for saguaro is *hahshani* and I thought again of the blood-colored wine made from the red fruit. The O'odham call the ironwood tree *ho'idkam*. Perhaps this should be the name of the new monument.

Sometimes our geology adventures would takes us past the mine and completely circumnavigate Ragged Top to come out near the old ghost town of Silverbell. Being geologists, of course the ruins of the old mining town interested us. The ruins of the smelter at Sasco still stand. There are also the stone masonry walls of what historians believed to have once been The Rockland Hotel. It was there that Mr. and Mrs. Charlie Coleman resided.

The Colemans had undergone an impromptu midnight marriage ceremony after fleeing a rigged poker game in Tombstone. The newlyweds hopped a train to Sasco and disembarked with suitcases full of money. They escaped by blending in with the crowd. We will probably never discover Mrs. Coleman's first or maiden name but we do know that she was regarded as a beautiful lady. She soon left Mr. Coleman for, not one but, two boyfriends.

Mr. Coleman began an abusive interrogation of his wife. The innkeeper arrived to tell Mr. Coleman to keep his hands off the lady and Mr. Coleman is said to have replied that she was no lady, she was his wife and he would do with her whatever he pleased. The innkeeper left, only to return shortly with his shotgun. He knocked on the door. When Mr. Coleman interrupted the beating of his wife to answer the door, the shotgun blasted Mr. Coleman dead. A jury of his peers found the innkeeper not guilty, claiming that Mr. Coleman was a drunk and a bully who needed killing.

Besides the smelter and the hotel there is not much left of Sasco and Silverbell except for a pair of graveyards. The cemetery at Sasco is beside an old ranch, where horses still stand inside the corral walls. The graves here are ornate and beautiful in accordance with Hispanic traditions. There is even a statue of the lady in blue. Walking around the graveyard I noticed two things. First, many of the graves dated to the great influenza epidemic of World War I. The tiny town of Sasco was not able to recover from the two-fisted blow of the mine closing and the influenza epidemic and soon closed down.

Sasco Cemetery – note the doll made of corn husk and human hair.

Second, the graveyard is littered with pottery. The spot chosen for this cemetery is part of the ancient Hohokam village of Cerro Prieto. It brings to mind the *palimpsest*; the notion of a landscape having layers and layers of people throughout history. Layers of stories and myths all emanate from the same landscape, all of them filtered by the unchanging terrain.

There is a second cemetery; belonging to the ghost town of Silverbell, around the backside of the mountain a little ways. This second cemetery is not as well tended or cared for. It consists mostly of stick crosses and no headstones besides a single piece of marble that announces the final resting place of Mary Ann O'Toole.

There was something surprising within the Silverbell cemeteries. There were small mounds of stones, tiny fresh graves only big enough to hold the bodies of newborns or stillborns. None of these graves held names but only tiny pieces of ribbons which declared *"la nina"* or *"nino"*. These new graves shocked and upset me and I pondered for a long time the reason for their existence. At last I came to an explanation, that these bereaved parents, probably so impoverished that they carried with them nothing but breath and hope, came to this abandoned cemetery to bury their newborn dead, children so tiny that they did not even own names. The loving parents knew that ancient bones were buried here and that even tiny children need a hand to hold and someone to show them the path into heaven.

Bear grass was used to make baskets by Native Americans. Some thick stands of bear grass have been harvested by the same tribes for centuries and centuries.

chapter 17:
Bear Grass Harvest

I was riding my bicycle along Cody Loop in Oracle on a blustery monsoon day in early August. I had pedaled past the end of the pavement and now my tires were rolling directly atop Mother Earth. As I struggled up a steep hill, I had plenty of time to observe the scenery. There was a large pickup truck at the top of the hill and along the side of the road there were bundles of green.

The bundles of green were loosely stacked in piles every 20 feet or so. Each bundle contained a couple dozen slender green stalks with white bases. Someone was harvesting the bear grass!

The question of who was harvesting the bear grass was answered quickly. There was a man and a woman just off the road, in a thicket of manzanita, scrub oak and, of course, they were in the midst of a stand of bear grass. The man was swinging a big heavy ax and the woman was gathering the bear grass into bundles. I stopped and introduced myself.

The woman replied, "I am Agatha and this is my brother Stanley."

Because of their dark brown skin and jet black hair, I asked respectfully if they were of Native American ancestry. Agatha replied that she and her brother were both from the Tohono O'odham reservation. Cody Loop in the little town of Oracle has been a traditional bear grass gathering place among the Tohono O'odham for centuries, perhaps for millennia stretching back to the Hohokam settlements which once thrived here.

Agatha, now middle aged, remembers being brought here as a little girl by her grandmother. Now Agatha and Stanley, brother and sister, keep the ancient family tradition alive. At the pickup truck, a younger brother and sister take a break, making use of the cold beverages in the cooler. Harvesting bear grass is hard work. Stanley raises the heavy ax above his head again and again, swinging it down with force into the clumps of bear grass, freeing them from the thick rich earth. Stanley swings the heavy ax again and again, with small grunts, panting for breath. It is one of the reasons Agatha does most of the talking.

Once the bear grass is harvested the hard work is just beginning. Agatha will use the bundles of bear grass for making baskets. The bear grass must be pulled apart, strand by strand, into individual fibers. The bear grass will be used to make the interior coil of the basket. Then the fibers of the banana yucca will complete the shell of the basket. Black threads are harvested from a bush called devil's claw. It is these black highlights that make the distinctive designs and figures of O'odham baskets.

I ask Agatha if she makes her baskets primarily for sale and she says indeed part of her incentive is financial. She does sell her baskets through some gift shops. Agatha also makes an equal portion for use around the home, and as gifts to friends and family for special occasions.

"I have not come here for five or six years," Agatha tells me. "There sure are a lot of traffic lights on Oracle Road nowadays and there were buildings that I don't ever remember being there before. Soon Tucson will stretch all the way to Oracle."

I cringe. Monsoon lightning flashes over the ridge. I ask Agatha and Stanley if they would mind if I wrote an article about them. Agatha consents. Stanley grunts his approval and continues swinging his big heavy ax, never breaking rhythm. I ask them if they would mind letting me take their picture for the newspaper.

Agatha giggles and confesses "No one has ever taken my photograph in my entire life, but sure, all right."

I admit that I must bicycle home and retrieve my camera before I can photograph them. I offer to bicycle home as quickly as I can and return with my camera.

Agatha sighs and says, "You can try but we are just about done here. We still need to head out to Willow Springs Road and harvest the yucca. Then it is a long drive home; a very long drive home."

I bicycle home as fast and breathless as I can manage. The rain starts to fall softly. I grab the camera, check to make sure there is film inside, hop in the car, and by the time I return they have departed. Lightning splits the horizon, as bright as any photo flash cube. Agatha survives another day without having her picture taken but, if the baskets she weaves are beautiful, one of them may end up surviving in a museum for centuries.

This statue is of a hoop and stick player (a traditional Apache gambling game) and is located outside the Apache Gold casino.

chapter 18:
Losing Geronimo's Language

"It is almost as if the Apache language comes from Mars because no one speaks it anymore," explained Edgar Perry. "How will you speak it when I am dead and gone to Mars? Don't be lazy – do the work. If our language dies, the spirit of our people dies, the culture of Geronimo dies."

Lecturing at the Arizona Historical Society (AHS) in 2004, Perry, a shaggy haired grandfather, began his presentation about language without words; using only paint and tissues. While the crowd waited for him to speak, there was only silence as he faced his canvas of heavy paper, back to the audience. He applied broad strokes of red, blue and yellow to the canvas.

"I am painting like I always do," Mr. Perry explained, speaking for the first time. "I am painting with acrylics and napkins. You should try it, you'll like it. It will release the little kid inside, and we are all little kids, just some of us have big bodies."

From the blur of bright colors swirling across the canvas, gradually a landscape of mountains, cacti, and sunset begins to emerge. Perry explains that his painting depicts the heart of the Dragoon Mountains, Cochise's Stronghold. "The name *Cochise*," Perry explains, "comes from the Apache words *Ko* and *Chiz*. *Ko* means fires and *Chiz* means wood, this is because Cochise earned his nickname by selling firewood to the soldiers as a young man.

Names are never a simple thing in Apache culture, they often carry their own histories. Edgar Perry was born 66 years ago in a wikiup in the White Mountains of Arizona, the oldest child of Mary Quintero Perry. The name Perry comes from a U.S. cavalry officer, Maj. David Perry who took a liking to two Apache scouts. To set them apart from other Apache scouts, he lent them his last name. One of those scouts was Perry's grandfather. Edgar Perry's grandmother was Helen Alchesay Perry, daughter of the legendary Apache chief Alchesay. Edgar Perry only recently retired as a teacher from Alchesay High School in Whiteriver, a school named after his valiant ancestor.

When the Apache were first confined on reservations, the U.S. government informed the people that they must have last names. Some, like Grandfather Perry, took their names from soldiers. Others named themselves after Mexican settlers and characters from the Bible. Some Apaches even picked last names at random from the phone book.

Other names, such as identification numbers, were more practical. The reservation agents often had a hard time telling one Apache from another and needed numbers to keep track of handing out rations. Perry's grandfather, one of the last Apache scouts, was number A-43 and his father V-70. Although Edgar Perry was not assigned a number, his illustrious ancestor Alchesay was A-1. I spent some tranquil sunsets fishing along the shores of A-1 lake long before I knew how it got its name.

Edgar Perry also has an Apache name. It is *Jaabilaatha*, which relates to his clan. It describes a stand of cottonwood trees where the Eagle clan originates. Among the Apache, lineal descent is reckoned through female relatives. The Whiteriver Apache have four clans; Bear, Butterfly, Eagle and Roadrunner. Edgar Perry is a member of the Eagle Clan.

It is where language touches the sacred and spiritual that issues of cultural sensitivity arise. Jon Reyhner, editor of the book *Teaching Indigenous Language*, published by Northern

Arizona University in 1997, includes a chapter by native speaker Bernadette Adley Santa-Maria entitled White Mountain Apache Language. She describes misgivings among some native speakers. "There are those who respect each other's beliefs and resent the continuous probing by outsiders who want answers and knowledge for curiosity's sake, for exploitation, or for research that does not benefit us. Our wise elders tell us that there are some things in this world best left uninvestigated, unsaid, and not revealed."

Her paper also revealed sharp disparity between generations. "Regarding Apache language ability, most (95 percent) respondents, 40 years and over, speak Apache . . . compared to only 28 percent of those under 30." What she found most disturbing was a pattern among children, parents, and grandparents. "More (43 percent) respond to parents/ guardians in Apache only, while fewer (28 percent) speak to their children/ grandchildren in Apache." If the children do not learn the language from their parents it will be difficult to preserve.

Edgar Perry is also a great proponent of speaking the language at home. He cites inroads made by the dominant culture. "Ten years ago, only 30 percent of high school students in Whiteriver could speak the language fluently," Perry says. Meanwhile, in the more isolated Cibecue, 50 miles away, 90 percent were fluent in Apache." Perry sees much of the decline coming from electronic media. Even the most isolated regions of the White Mountain reservation have television, DVD players, rap music, and the internet.

"Everything's in English," Perry complains. When parents ask him how to instill the Apache culture and language in their children, he says, "I tell them to turn off the TV and to speak in Apache all the time."

Perry explains that his mother and father were wed in a traditional arranged marriage and although they did not love each other; they still produced ten children. "Just shows what you can get accomplished when you are not distracted by television."

Sometimes the media is part of the solution and not the problem. Radio Station KNNB has been broadcasting as the voice of White Mountain Apache Radio for more than 20 years. The call letters have special meaning. K is the FCC mandate for all stations west of the Mississippi River. The NNB stands for the Apache words *Ndee nitch'i binagodie*. *Ndee* is the word the people use to name themselves (*Apache* was the name given to them by the Spanish) and *nitchi'i binagodie* means "a place where you report to the people."

Each morning, the station begins the broadcast with traditional Native American music and then switches to a locally produced country-music show. There are also news shows on local issues such as education and health. There are syndicated national-news shows such as National Public Radio but about three-quarters of the airwave time is dedicated to music. KNNB sees the radio station as an important tool for preserving the language and encourages the use of Apache by its on air personalities. Station manager Vangee Natan is aware of the danger of too many lessons and too much talk. "People will shut us out."

During the massive Rodeo Chedeski fire, KNNB extended its broadcasts from 18 to 24 hours a day. The newspaper *Indian Country Today* described it: "It was a frightening time. Smoke blanketed the valleys." At one point the station broadcast directly to Hon Dah Casino telling people they had one hour to evacuate. "People were coming on the radio in Apache and giving information on the fire," said Katy Aday.

"To hear it coming from our elders in Apache, it helped a lot."

On Sunday, one of the KNNB programming highlights is the obituaries. Program hosts read 60-second tributes while the deceased's favorite music is played in the background. Most of Sunday's programming is dominated by religious programs, especially Bible readings in Apache. I am reminded of a church in the tiny town of Whiteriver which features a sign of an Apache warrior on horseback with a Bible tucked under his arm and holding the cross like a spear. Over the years I have photographed that colorful sign many times. It seems like, in every picture, the horse is a different color.

Edgar Perry uses a religious term to illustrate a point about fluency. Almost all Apache, even those who know only one or two words of the language, know that the word for Christian is *iinashoogld*. Not all Apaches know the word comes from two smaller words meaning "dragging shirt," a reference to the robed, Spanish missionaries who were the Apache's first exposure to the Christian religion.

In her paper, Adler discusses levels of fluency as a way to connect with deeper levels of culture. She explains that language is more than vocabulary, spelling and grammar. "I viewed the Apache language as interconnected with all aspect of the Apache society rather than the minutiae we always focused on. As our work became more complex, I began to articulate that there is more to consider in speaking Apache and I began relating some of the beliefs, attitudes and opinions of Apache speakers about their language that put much more meaning contextually into the syntax and structure of speech."

Adler also recognized the value of taping oral histories.

WHITERIVER

Church sign on the White Mountain Apache reservation in northern Arizona

"Written and video and audio recordings of our languages should be done for our tribal archives and future generations of Apaches." Edgar Perry had similar experiences with oral histories. "We would take a tape recorder out and record the old people. But when we went to translate them, we didn't know how to phonetically write the Apache language. With all those beautiful, taped stories, we decided to write a dictionary."

Just once, I stumbled upon an oral-history transcription in progress. I had visited the Mogollon ruins at Kinnishba and drove to the Fort Apache Cultural Museum (founded by Edgar Perry) to ask for some information. I interrupted two nice ladies who were transcribing from a large reel-to-reel tape machine, I could hear just enough to realize the voice on tape was not speaking English. I requested some information about Kinnishba and one of the women was kind enough to run to the back room and copy some material for me. While I waited, a gentleman and his friend entered the museum. The gentleman introduced himself as Keith Basso. He said that he had been working on an atlas for years; an atlas of the Apache lands using Apache names.

It was a serendipitous moment that I remembered for many years. He was bursting with pride, smiling big beneath his cowboy hat, wearing jeans and boots. The two Apache women were overwhelmed by the generosity of the gift. Later, I would discover that Keith Basso's book *Wisdom*

Sits in Places won the Western States book award for creative nonfiction. *Wisdom Sits in Places* is more than just a book about the Apache language. It also tells the story of that atlas. Basso found that almost all Apache place names imply looking at the place from a specific viewpoint. These viewpoints are linked with specific stories, stories associated with that particular place and all of them not only relate an Apache history to the area but also layer the landscape with a quilt of moral values, displaying what it is to be Apache.

One of the examples Basso uses in the book is when he observes four elders sitting on a porch during a tranquil summer evening. One of the Apache grandmothers mentions that her brother has a gambling problem. To show their empathy, the others mention a succession of places. The place names are all associated with stories whose basic moral can be summed up as "a fool and his money are soon parted." Thus the land itself becomes a shorthand code which conveys both tribal history and a moral code. Quite an atlas indeed.

People interested in hearing the Apache language for themselves can listen to KNNB whenever they drive through Whiteriver (190 miles north of Tucson). They can also watch Ron Howard's western movie *The Missing*. During the course of the movie the actors speak lines in three languages; English, Spanish, and Apache. The dialect is Chiricuahua so it is slightly different than the White Mountain version spoken by Edgar Perry and his neighbors.

Fluent speakers of Chiricuhua Apache are said to number only in the hundreds. Tommy Lee Jones said one of the reasons he agreed to perform in the movie was the challenge of acting in three different languages. The special features section of the DVD version has a chapter displaying the Apache language lessons.

In an effort to keep Apache traditional values and customs alive, Perry has founded a troop of Gaan, the lively crowned dancers of Apache festivals. He and his dance troupe have performed all across the nation and throughout the world, including many of the capitals of Europe. Perry closes his lecture by mentioning some upcoming dance dates in North Dakota. "Of course we will fly there," Edgar chuckles, "We are the Eagle Clan."

chapter 19:
Arizona's Mammoth Hunters

It is hard to imagine that this expanse of saguaros, ocotillo, cactus and grass was once marsh lands, lakes, and conifer forests. It is hard to believe that only 10,000 years ago mammoths thundered across this particular part of the earth, but they did. The story of the mammoth-hunting Native Americans, the very first Native Americans in what is now southern Arizona and Cochise County, is a fascinating tale.

Maybe as many as 50,000 years ago, during a great ice age, Asian nomads crossed the frozen Bering Strait into Alaska and began to populate the North American continent. Archaeologists now believe there were three great waves of migrations into the New World. The first two migrations did not make much progress but the third wave of immigrants invented a new projectile point technology which allowed them to hunt big game. These points were named after the location of their discovery; Clovis, New Mexico, the people who used them are known as Clovis Men.

Arizona was a hotbed of Clovis activity. Three major excavations of mammoth-kill sites are located in Cochise County. It was at the Naco site in 1951, when projectile points were discovered embedded in the fossil mammoth bones, that scientists were able to prove that mammoth hunters once lived in Arizona. Once the first discovery was made, it seemed to open a floodgate of mammoth-hunter sites.

Rancher Ed Lehner showed up at the Naco dig and told the University of Arizona crew that they might want to check out some of the heavily eroded arroyos on his land. At Lehner's Ranch the archaeologists discovered more projectile points associated with mammoths as well as the remains of bison, horses, and tapirs. Lehner's Ranch, as well as nearby Murray Springs, showed projectile points, game animals, and ancient hearths containing fossilized scorched bones.

Both of these sites, Lehner Ranch and Murray Springs are open for unguided tours. It gave me chills to walk the ground at Murray Springs, the same earth the fur-clad, spear-toting, mammoth-hunting warriors once tread. The map we had obtained at the San Pedro House allowed us to identify where the hearths were located. Ten thousand years ago nomadic clans gathered before roaring fires in the hearths and sang, danced, and celebrated successful mammoth hunts. Life must have been good for the Clovis men, the population of Native Americans soared and Clovis projectile points have been discovered all across the continent.

The large game of the Ice Age provided a bountiful larder. The North American bestiary included the woolly mammoth, American mastodon, giant sloth, wild horse, a four-pronged antelope, camel, glyptodont, a 300-pound beaver, and a giant bison. There was plenty of competition from other predators too. These include the dire wolf, the saber-toothed cat, the American lion (hundreds of pounds heavier than his African cousin), and the short-faced bear, who was much larger than today's grizzly.

The main problem facing the Clovis Men was a gradually changing climate. As the Ice Age retreated, the big game moved northwards with it. Some Clovis Men followed it, but others adapted to the changing environment. It was out of these adaptations that the Cochise Culture arose. The Cochise Culture was a plant-harvesting people. Although they did not farm, wild plants became the mainstay of their diet.

Archaeological digs associated with the Cochise Culture have produced grinding tools and other stone implements for processing plant foods. The Cochise people were among the first to make baskets. Duck decoys and nets, for hunting small game such as rabbits, have also been found among their remains. A great deal of historical debate has arisen as to whether the Cochise people were related to the Clovis Men. Although many Cochise village sites existed simultaneously with Clovis sites, no archeological excavation has yet turned up both Clovis points and Cochise plant processing tools.

Experts debate whether the people of the plants and the big-game hunters were the same people, with different camps for different seasons. They debate whether they were two distinct, separate cultures who rarely interacted as they pursued different natural resources.

Esteemed archaeologist Dr. Emil Haury believed that the answers to these questions might possibly be discovered beneath the sands of the Wilcox Playa. Ten thousand years ago this playa was a prehistoric lake known to scientists as Lake Cochise. Ancient human bones have been discovered along the sandy shores. It is the only place in the southwest where the tool kits of both Clovis and Cochise cultures have been found close to each other, but not yet definitively linked.

Imagine the scene of over a thousand years ago as a Native American bow hunter stalks a deer in the White Mountains, creeping up silently with a bag of corn pollen around his neck. Archeologists believe that, as the climate warmed, the Clovis Men retreated with the big-game animals up into the Mogollon Rim country of what is now Arizona and New Mexico. It was out of the Arizona Clovis Men that the Mogollon culture began to arise about 200 AD.

The Mogollon supported themselves mostly with venison and antelope and by harvesting many of the same wild foods as their ancestors from the Cochise Culture. They also practiced small-scale farming; growing corn, beans, and squash. The Mogollon were an inventive people, becoming the first culture in the southwest to have pottery and bow and arrows and to plant corn. However they still relied mostly on their hunting skills to provide their diet.

During the centuries of 700 to 900 AD the climate of the southwest was particularly wet. During these years the Mogollon returned almost exclusively to hunting as a food source; disregarding farming altogether.

The later Mogollon phases, starting about 900 AD, saw a greater and greater influence by the Anasazai. The Mogollon began to build above ground pueblos and place a greater emphasis on farming. Many of these brick pueblos can be visited today, including those in the Mimbres Valley of New Mexico, Grasshopper and Point of Pines in Arizona, and my very favorite, Kinishba on the White Mountain Apache Reservation.

Kinishba is an Apache word translated roughly as "brown house." This large stone building is located in the heart of the Sawtooth Mountains and is a masterpiece of Mogollon architecture. During the height of its occupancy thousands of people called Kinishba home. Archaeologists found many fascinating things at Kinishba including one room which seemed to serve as a pottery museum, holding only shards of wonderfully detailed, intricately painted pottery.

There is a courtyard in the back of the multi-storied building where one can stand and imagine the scene when priests stood before a stone altar. This altar was decorated with a kachina dancer adorned with rain and sun masks, lightning bolts in either hand, and flanked by corn stalks. On top of the altar would be brightly painted deer and antelope jaws. The Hopi, who feel they are descended from the peoples at Kinishba, still send elderly priests to the brown brick house ruins to leave offerings of hawk feathers and prayers.

It puts shivers up and down my spine to stand in the Kinnishba courtyard and imagine the scene of about a thousand years ago when drums and dancers filled the plaza, just as it gives me thrills to stand on the ground at Murray Springs and picture what it was like 10,000 years ago when the Clovis men were hunting mammoths and filling the continent with the first Native Americans.

Kinnishba

Casa Grande Monument

chapter 20:
Casa Grande and the Grewe Complex

The large adobe castle was already crumbling into ruins when Father Kino named it *Casa Grande* or "Big House" on November 27, 1694. Kino offered the first written description: "The Casa Grande is a four-story building, as large as a castle, and equal to the largest church in these lands of Sonora." The exploring friar improvised an altar and performed Mass, the first time Casa Grande was used as a temple in centuries.

When Frank Hamilton Cushing arrived in 1887, he declared right away that the large, imposing, adobe castle and accompanying platform mounds were signs of a stratified society ruled by an elite group of priests.

Kino was also the first to speculate on the origins of the people who built Casa Grande. "It is said that the ancestors of Montezuma deserted and depopulated it. Beset by neighboring Apaches, they left for the east. From there they turned toward the south and southwest, finally founding the great city and court of Mexico ... There are seven or eight more of these large ancient houses and ruins of whole cities, with many broken *metates* and jars, charcoal etc. These certainly must be the Seven Cities mentioned by the holy man Fray Marcos De Niza."

Just like that, Kino had tied this very real ruin to two of the Spaniards favorite myths; Aztlan the fabled homeland of the Aztecs and the Seven Cities of Cibola searched for by the massive Coronado expedition.

Archaeologists now believe that the transfer of culture went in the other direction. They believe that the rich and inventive people of Mexico sent a class of astronomer priests to colonize the people on their northern frontier. The great house at Casa Grande was completed around 1350 when the Hohokam people were concentrating their population around several riverine cities.

The timbers used to build the adobe castle, juniper, pine and fir, do not grow in the surrounding desert but were floated more than 60 miles down the Gila River from the nearest mountains. Saguaro ribs were stretched across the beams and all of it was covered with adobe. The walls are four feet thick and the building is four stories tall. It took more than 3,000 tons of adobe to finish Casa Grande.

After Kino, many other non-natives came to visit Casa Grande. In 1697 Captain Cristobal Martin Bernal came and visited the ruins, noticing the canals. It is not known for certain who was the first American to see the ruins but most likely it was a mountain man. Rugged explorers such as Joseph Reddeford Walker, Ewing Young, and James Ohio Pattie all trapped beaver on the Gila River. One mountain man, Pauline Weaver, carved his first initial and last name into the adobe; "P. Weaver, 183_" (the last number is illegible).

In 1846, General Kearny's army, making their historic march from Saint Louis to Southern California, stopped by to sketch the ruins and write descriptions. The sketches by the artist John Mix Stanley are among the best ever drawn of the great adobe castle. The next official visitor was John Russell Bartlett who came through in 1852, trying to survey the new Mexican – American border as set out by the war of 1848.

As any Arizonan will tell you, July 12th is the wrong day to spend at Casa Grande. Bartlett described the day, "After three hours spent at the ruins, the hottest I think I have ever experienced, the mercury in the shade beneath the trees was 119 degrees Fahrenheit."

The completion of the Southern Pacific railroad brought

tourists in droves. By the 1880s, visitors began to note extensive vandalism. A series of excavations were led at Casa Grande by some of the early heroes of American archaeology, men such as Bandelier, Cushing, and Fewkes. In 1889, the ruins at Casa Grande were set aside as America's first archeological preserve.

In 1969, John Molloy demonstrated that many of the openings along the high walls could be used to observe celestial events such as solar equinoxes and solstices. Casa Grande was almost certainly set up as a huge astronomical observatory and temple, housing an elite class of astronomer priests. Although this site was occupied for centuries and centuries, the adobe castle of Casa Grande has become synonymous with this village. A fair comparison would be with the spectacular cliff dwellings at Mesa Verde, even though those pueblos represent only the last century and a half out of a millennia of residence.

The huge, adobe astronomical tower at Casa Grande represented only one of the last stages of a long series of native-desert civilizations. During the course of centuries, this village gradually migrated eastward. Archaeologists commonly refer to the largest of these earlier incarnations as the Grewe Site. Grewe was excavated by Julian Hayden in 1931 and most recently by D. Craig in the 1990s. Grewe was occupied from 500 to 1100 AD. Typical of many ancient cities, houses were built on top of houses. There was one particular cluster of 13 adobe homes that was continuously occupied for more than 200 years, surviving as an entity approximately as long as our nation has existed.

One would expect such a long occupation to leave behind a wealth of material possessions. The archaeologists were not disappointed, discovering more than 400,000 pottery shards. Most of these pottery shards are classic Hohokam red on buff and many feature the bird motifs common to Hohokam ceramics. During his excavations, Julian Hayden also discovered elaborate pendants featuring a religious deity or bird nosed shaman. These pendants have been traced to Zacatecas deep in Mexico; hundreds of miles to the south. Zacatecas was undergoing a religious revival at the time, centered on religious architecture. Casa Grande may have participated in or been influenced by events in Zacatecas.

The arrival of the great ballgame to the Hohokam dates to this period. Nearly all Hohokam villages feature at least one ball court in a prominent location and it is believed that the ballgames promoted unity and trade. At some Hohokam villages, ceramic figurines of heavily tattooed ball players have been found.

Somewhere around 1100 AD, the daisy cluster of mud pueblos around Grewe were abandoned and the whole village migrated to the east. Archaeologists are not certain what prompted this move but it was accompanied by several important cultural changes. Construction on the great castle of Casa Grande was also begun. The ball courts were abandoned during this period. The network of irrigation canals became much longer and more elaborate. The population in the city of Casa Grande increased greatly during this period and, as the kingdom grew, the reliance upon corn in the diet grew. The increased importance of astronomy to such a culture is in keeping with this transformation to an agriculturally based society.

By the time Father Kino arrived in 1694, the village at Casa Grande was mostly abandoned with only a few scattered families remaining. No one is certain exactly why the civilization at Casa Grande was abandoned. Seeking answers, Julian Hayden turned his attentions to the oral traditions of the O'odham. The O'odham do not call it Casa Grande but *Blue Hawk's Castle* or *Morning Blue's Castle*, depending on the translation.

Morning Blue was supposed to be a powerful king who had a right-hand man; an astronomer priest named Yellow Buzzard. Morning Blue was not only the king of Casa Grande but of a kingdom where the realm included several of these magic houses which served as both temple and astronomical observatory.

The power of Yellow Buzzard lay in his ability to predict total eclipses of the sun. According to some of the oral histories, the castle at Casa Grande was surrounded by a moat which held Morning Blue's pet sea monster. You have to love a legend which includes both saguaros and sea monsters. Morning Blue's pet was said to be the love child of Quetzacoatl, the plumed serpent of Mesoamerica, and the nehbig, the sea monster who used to live in the prehistoric lake which once stretched from Quitovac in Mexico to Quitobaquito in Organ Pipe National Monument.

According to books written by Pimas, George Webb and Anna Moore Shaw, Morning Blue was a cruel and terrible tyrant. The stories are filled with tales of his armies marching across the desert to collect tributes of corn and turquoise and kidnapping the daughters of local citizens. Naturally, the reign of Morning Blue was not popular with the local people.

In some of the tales, Casa Grande falls because of mischievous Coyote. The siege at Casa Grande had become a long and painful stalemate when Coyote convinced Old Man Badger that Casa Grande was the largest prairie dog den he had ever seen. Old Man Badger is famous for being nearsighted and he fell for Coyote's ruse. Badger dug beneath the castle walls and the invading army followed, breaching the defenses.

Morning Blue turned to Yellow Buzzard, seeking shamanic help. Yellow Buzzard said that if they cut open his chest and sacrificed his heart; the kingdom would be saved.

Morning Blue protested but Yellow Buzzard insisted. When they cut open the wizard astronomer's chest, there was no heart at all, only a large green stone. When Julian Hayden was collecting oral histories in the 1960s, one of the elders showed him the giant green crystal (Hayden believed it to be peridot) that was removed from Yellow Buzzard's chest.

As the invading army fought their way past the last of the defenders, Morning Blue climbed to the top of the Casa Grande and held the stone above his head. The stone did nothing. The invaders soon overran the village and Morning Blue was barely able to escape. Morning Blue fled to the next city in his kingdom.

The invading army followed in hot pursuit and once again the defenders were overwhelmed. Once again, Morning Blue sought magical aid from the green stone and nothing happened. Morning Blue and his followers fled to the next city and the invading army chased them across the desert. Finally, Morning Blue and his followers were in the last city in the kingdom. Morning Blue and his army were backed up against the shores of the lake which stretched from Quitobaquito to Quitovac. With nowhere else to run, Morning Blue held the green stone above his head one last time.

The giant chunk of peridot caught the sun and twinkled, waking up something deep in the bottom of the lake. The *nehbig*, the mother of the sea monster in Morning Blue's moat, noticed the stone. Like a bass drawn to a lure, she rose from the bottom of the lake. Imagine the surprise of the invading army, just as they were about to capture Morning Blue and secure total victory, the sea serpent raised its head. The nehbig swallowed the invaders whole. Then the nehbig swallowed Morning Blue and his followers as well.

Next the nehbig sank to the bottom of the lake and took a nap, sleeping on his full belly. While the nehbig slept, and she slept for a very long time, she grew. When the nehbig awoke she was large enough to raise her head above the water and suck all the deer and bighorn sheep down from the mountains. After eating another full meal, the nehbig napped and grew some more. When the nehbig awoke again she was big enough to suck down entire villages, swallowing the O'odham people in great big gulps.

Desperate, the people went to seek out Elder Brother Iiyotoi and request his aid. Iiyotoi asked to borrow the large chunk of peridot. Elder Brother marched to the edge of the prehistoric lake and held the green stone above his head. The nehbig woke and raised her sea monster head above the waters, preparing to swallow Iiyotoi. Iiyotoi took one of the slender ribs from a saguaro and leapt inside the gaping mouth of the sea monster. He used the saguaro rib to prop open the jaws of the nehbig so she could not close her mouth. As Iiyotoi crawled down the gullet of the beast he got his obsidian knife ready. Then to his surprise he discovered not one but two hearts.

Iiyotoi cut out both hearts. The nehbig began to thrash about and wail in terrible agony. Iiyotoi barely escaped.

According to O'odham legends all that thrashing around emptied most of the water from the lake. That is why today, Quitobaquito Springs is a tiny pond surrounded by large mud flats where the lake used to extend. The mud flats are filled with prehistoric bones (including mammoth, camel, and giant ground sloth); these bones are said to be former dinner victims of the nehbig.

The two hearts Iiyotoi cut from the monster were hidden in a cave and a minor international scandal erupted. During the Mexican Revolution, one of Pancho Villa's soldiers stole one of the hearts and sold it for money to buy weapons and ammunition. During the 1920s a large tooth, measuring 12 inches long was discovered in the Quitobaquito mud. It was proof, the O'odham claimed, of the *nehbig* who used to live there.

In his prize winning essay, *When The Spring Of Animal Dreams Runs Dry*, Gary Paul Nabhan describes the moment when an O'odham elder placed the heart of the nehbig in his hands. Nabhan says the heart was a giant bone. When he was temporarily left alone with the artifact, he was tempted to chip off a flake and smuggle it out so that scientists could test it and discover what species the bone belonged to or even discover a new species. On the mud flats of an ancient lake filled with prehistoric bones, who knew what kind of specimen had been saved and celebrated as something unique and sacred. In the end, Nabhan decided to leave the mystery in the hands of the elders.

Artifacts from the tale of Morning Blue litter the Sonoran landscape. They include the string of magic houses such as Casa Grande, the green stone shown to Julian Hayden in Sacaton, the giant tooth found in the Quitobaquito mud, the nehbig heart held by Gary Nabhan and the stolen nehbig heart rumored to be hidden somewhere in Germany.

There is still one more artifact which tells this tale.

Many Hohokam village sites feature petroglyphs of stick-figure men climbing up the rocks they are carved into. These rock carvings tell part of the story of Yellow Buzzard. Not only could Yellow Buzzard predict eclipses but these eclipses were omens of floods. It was during this period that many Hohokam villages were moved from valleys to the hilltops. Our science says a relationship between eclipses and floods is nonexistent. However, archaeologists have compared the astronomical data with the rainfall record and discovered that the years following total eclipses were indeed years when the Gila and Salt Rivers crested their banks.

chapter 21:
Romo Cache Petroglyphs

I searched for some time before I found them. I talked to lots of people who had discovered the Romo Cache petroglyphs and all of them assured me they were easy to find. Every one of them repeated the same vague directions; locating them somewhere between The Cottonwoods and Catalina State Park. I had been assured by a park ranger that this was the largest set of petroglyphs in the entire Santa Catalina Mountain range. I kept searching, getting scratched by the underbrush as I wandered in the wilderness. Once, I startled a deer at the top of a narrow rocky gorge. The deer bounded away and where the deer had been standing I saw a rock panel adorned with petroglyphs. This single panel contained no more than a half-dozen symbols etched into the rock. Most prominent of these symbols was a spiral which ended with an arrow at the tail. I suspected this symbol was telling me where to find something but I had no idea how to follow the directions.

The main set of petroglyphs eluded me for the longest time until I stumbled upon them while I was looking for something else. First, I came across a set of boulders encoded with wavy lines and symbols believed to be phosphenes, the images produced by the optic nerves when the mind is in an altered state of consciousness. These altered states of consciousness can be arrived at through hallucinogenic plants or they can be self induced by fasting or sleep deprivation.

At this first grouping of Native American rock art there are many panels scattered across a field of boulders. There is one panel which uses the technique of rock incorporation. Rock incorporation involves using the shape and features of the rock itself to blend in with the pictures. In this case, a prominent knob sticks out from the boulder and is surrounded by a series of concentric circles, possibly denoting a near by hill and surrounding countryside.

The Native Americans who etched these petroglyphs were most likely the Hohokam. Although there are a variety of prehistoric sites in the Catalina State Park vicinity they usually are lumped together under the archaeological label of the Romero Ruins, named after the largest village in the neighborhood. This site appears to have been continuously inhabited from 500 until 1450 AD and abandoned shortly before the arrival of Columbus. The highest population

Romo Cache petroglyph

was about 300 residents from 850 to 1000 AD. Archaeologists speculate that during these years the Sutherland Wash probably flowed year round, providing lots of water for irrigation and farming. After 1150 AD, the entire village was surrounded by a stone wall. This implies a need for protection from attack and warfare.

Excavating Romero Ruins, the archaeologists found the usual artifacts associated with Hohokam inhabitants – pottery, metates, and seashell jewelry. The most common plant remains were corn, mesquite pods, and palo verde seeds. Signs of squash and *agave* were also found. Since agave does not grow naturally at this elevation it was most likely cultivated on the slopes of nearby terraced hillsides. Bones discovered in the trash piles revealed clues about the hunting habits of the Romero Ruin residents. Their diet included deer, bighorn sheep, jack rabbit, cottontail rabbit, pronghorn antelope, quail and some reptiles. The predominance of rabbit bones suggests that this was the main meat source for the tribe.

There are two large depressions at the site of the Romero Ruins that are believed to be ball courts. These ball courts are a clue to the strong links the Hohokam peoples had with cultures deep in Mexico where such ball courts originated. Some of the first Spanish explorers were able to chronicle their eyewitness accounts of these athletic events by watching the Aztecs play. A similar game is featured in the book of Mayan creation *The Popol Vuh*.

The game was played in a court dug out beneath the ground. There was a single hoop (like a basketball hoop only turned sideways) in the center of the field. There were two teams who contested for a small ball. The players were not allowed to use their arms but propelled the ball with their feet, and buttocks. The game was full contact.

It was traditional for team captains to be beheaded. For games on religious holidays, entire teams were sacrificed. These same Spanish chroniclers noted that outside the stadiums there were piles of skulls numbering in the thousands.

There is absolutely no evidence that the Hohokam culture engaged in human sacrifice. When a culture is struggling to survive in a desert, sacrificing your most athletic young men does not make sense. Hohokam villages all across Arizona have ball courts. Tiny Romero Ruins had two ball courts with cobblestone and plaster walls. It was an impressive allocation of communal labor for a tiny village. Most likely the residents of all the nearby hamlets came to help in the construction of the ball courts.

These ball courts had religious, economic, and social importance. The games were attended with a great deal of ceremony and ritual, frequently coinciding with holidays.

Villages would play other villages and this provided a chance for economic and social interchange. The nearest village with a ball court was only three miles away, across the valley at Honeybee Village. No doubt, Romero and Honeybee had a hotly contested local rivalry. The ball courts were sunken into the earth to allow large crowds to watch from above. It is easy to imagine a crowd jostling along the rim and cheering on the local sports heroes. Afterwards there would be the opportunity for people to renew acquaintances and engage in commerce.

Despite the importance of the ball courts in Hohokam culture, there are no known petroglyphs of the games or game players. The most common petroglyph symbol in the southwest is probably the ubiquitous goat. Upstream from the phosphene petroglyphs, following the narrow rock canyon to a small waterfall, are the main set of petroglyphs. These petroglyphs, located in this lovely location with waterfalls and cottonwood trees, consist mainly of goats. Some of the rock panels have numerous goats, each of them slightly different from the next, many of them accompanied by stick-figure men. On a rock face that looks down steeply on the water is a single large goat. The square shaped torso measures two and a half feet across and the artist went to great trouble to color in the body. The petroglyphs of the goats begin near the base of a small pool. They form a chain of goats culminating in the rock face with 14 goats that appear to be racing towards the next rock where the largest goat petroglyph sits all by itself. Just beyond that single goat petroglyph is a large boulder which has split in half.

The separated halves of this egg-shaped boulder provide just enough space for a few people at a time to climb inside. On the inside of the cracked boulder are a small handful of badly weathered petroglyph symbols including a few goats. On the outside of this cracked boulder are numerous petroglyphs, including two elaborate panels with intricate symbols and figures carved into the granite. One of these anthropomorphic figures I can only describe as some sort of kachina horned toad.

The meaning of such specific figures I will leave for you to interpret. With rock sites numbering in the tens of thousands in just Arizona alone, Native Americans were an extremely literate people. Like any literature, petroglyph symbols are meant to communicate a variety of meanings in a layered and diverse set of contexts. Meso-American scholars are just beginning to decipher the complex glyph script of the Mayans. I sincerely hope that the keys to interpreting petroglyphs only await further study. What I do know for certain is that searching for petroglyph sites, and trying to understand them, forces me to be aware of the land and the people who once lived here.

In the year 1949, a discovery was made by a deer hunter which gave this petroglyph site its name. Ray Romo was hunting along the steep slopes of the Santa Catalinas, struggling for footing among the loose talus and scree. Suddenly Romo felt his foot sink into the earth. Moving some of the loose rocks aside to investigate, Mr. Romo discovered that he had nearly crushed a clay bowl. The bowl was covering a ceramic jar and the jar was holding what noted archaeologist Emil Haury referred to as "the village strongbox."

The Romo Cache consisted of thousands of stone and shell beads and 30 copper bells. This is an amazing amount of accumulated wealth for such a tiny village. To string all the beads together in a single necklace would take more than 300 feet of thread. To drill and shape all the beads would be more work than one person could do in five or six years. The seashell beads came from the distant Sea of Cortez and the shores of the Pacific Ocean.

The copper bells were traded from central Mexico; the Native Americans of this area did not possess the technology to cast such bells. Although not unheard of in the southwest, such bells are rare. In the entire region there were only 620 copper bells at 90 sites. These sites are scattered unevenly and many contained only one bell. Only a few sites possess as many as ten copper bells. With 30 copper bells and the huge number of beads, the Romo Cache represents a massive store of prehistoric wealth.

Are the petroglyphs and the Romo Cache connected to this treasure in any way beyond proximity? No one knows for certain. Of course, both were created by the same villagers. If the glyphs at the waterfall were used in hunting rituals then it would have been ironic that a deer hunter discovered the secret of the lost treasure. Then again the petroglyph site might have been used in individual curing ceremonies or to celebrate a girl's first menstruation. Speculation is one of the most entertaining parts of petroglyph interpretation. It forces one to try to view Native American culture from a variety of viewpoints.

Was the treasure connected to the petroglyphs in any way? Did any of the glyphs serve as a map on how to find the treasure? Was the Romo Cache hidden where it was because it was a good hiding place and nothing more? Perhaps the wealth was hidden to save it from raiding nomads or the taxes and tribute demanded by the tyrant atop his throne at Casa Grande.

Sometimes my imagination runs wild and I can't help wondering if the petroglyphs and all those goats weren't a setting for hunters' rituals and male bonding. If that was the case then, men being men, they probably came to this petroglyph site before important ball games. Perhaps it is just my civic pride letting my imagination run wild, but isn't it possible that the local sports heroes kicked a lot of ball court booty. As their reputations grew and teams traveled farther to compete against local champions, the wagers would have grown larger and larger until . . . they grew to the size of the Romo Cache.

There is no archaeological evidence at all to support this theory but, since so much of prehistory is hidden in clouds of mystery. Go Team Go!

These Hohokam petroglyphs were discovered near a prehistoric treasure.

Chuckwalla

chapter 22:
The Lizardmobile

Some houses are haunted, and graveyards always seem to be inhabited by wispy spirits. When I was growing up, our 1968 Chevy Malibu had its own resident demon. The large lizard that lived in our car was kept plump by the popcorn I stuffed between the seats. My parents had no idea why the lizard lurked in our car, but I knew.

I knew because I was the one who accidentally unleashed him. Unlike most Gothic tales of poltergeists or demonic possession this haunting involved no black-magic ritual or tortured souls with unfinished business. The culprit was a birthday cake.

My mother had dragged me along while she visited a friend. As they conversed I scrambled out the back door. Beyond the gate was a wonderland of arroyo, alley, discarded junk, and garden. It was enough to keep a lad occupied for hours.

I scored big, unwittingly opening Pandora's Box by catching a lizard. Not just any lizard but a *chuckwalla*. Chuckwallas are among my favorite lizards because they are especially ugly and barbaric looking, often portraying monsters in the kind of low budget movies that were frequently shown on Sunday Afternoon Science Fiction Theater.

My plan was to take the lizard back home and re-release him in our backyard. From the trash scattered in the alley I was able to find a coffee can, some plastic wrap, and a rubber band. I used a broken pencil to punch some holes in the plastic wrap.

Certain that my mother would not approve, I took steps to conduct the maneuvers in secrecy. I climbed into the back seat of our car, holding the can down low where my mother would be unable to see it. It was then that my plan was foiled. Even though my mother's birthday was still three days away, her friend had presented her with a birthday cake.

"Here hold this," mother said as she thrust the cake into the back seat.

Not wanting to confess to having kidnapped a lizard, I dropped the coffee can to the floor and accepted the birthday cake. When we arrived home I hurriedly gave the cake back to my mother and checked the can.

It was empty.

The longer the lizard lived in the car, the longer the lizard became. From time to time it would make an unexpected appearance. Suddenly, it would dart out from beneath the front seat and make a mad dash through the forest of human legs, swerving between the brake and gas pedals. My mother would shriek; rapidly exiting the flow of traffic in order to ask bewildered gas station attendants to search her car for the renegade reptile. Other times, only the tip of a tail would poke out from beneath a seat to let you know that there was a hidden beast lurking in the car. Most of the time the lizard only let his presence be known by the sounds his claws made scratching against metal while he scurried about the automobile. No one ever actually saw the lizard when they were looking for him, so hunting for him turned out to be futile. Attempts to leave the car doors open and allow the lizard to emigrate on his own also turned out to be unsuccessful.

After all, why would the lizard want to leave? Chuckwallas are rock lizards and an automobile provided plenty of crevices to crawl into, all snug and secure. There was plenty to eat – fast food scraps, picnic leftovers – and even a few cake crumbs. Even if I couldn't confess to ownership, I loved my lizard. Every time my parents bought me popcorn, I made sure to shove some between the cushions of the backseat, helping the lizard grow long and fat. I used to ask for popcorn a lot.

Sometimes as we drove around town or on the highway, the sounds of the lizard dashing about under the seats seemed to last an extraordinarily long time. I wondered what made the lizard so busy. Perhaps he had acquired enough kernels to start a popcorn plantation under the back seat.

Grave of James McAvoy at the Oracle Cemetery.

chapter 23:
The Prospector

Recently I moved to the quaint little town of Oracle, Arizona, on the edge of the Santa Catalina Mountains. As I was exploring my new home town I wandered the local cemetery, or *"cementery"* as the mislabeled trash cans call it. It is a beautiful grave yard. Many of the graves are decorated in the traditions of Mexican folk art. There are many paper, plastic, and real flowers. There is the headstone of a famous writer.

The bodies are scattered across the hillside, forcing visitors to follow a meandering path through an oak forest filled with scrub jays and rabbits. Tucked in one corner, at the base of a gnarled tree trunk, is a tombstone that reads *"James McAvoy – prospector and friend"* It lists his date of birth as 1889 and the place as Ireland. This is one Celt buried a long way from home.

You have to wonder what it would take to lure a man to leave behind his native land and family and be willing to end up dying here alone. In this case, the mystery is solved by the tombstone. James McAvoy was a prospector.

Some men, when they get the thirst for gold in their blood they can think of nothing else. Who knows what tales James McAvoy had heard about the American frontier? Perhaps he had a grandfather or great-great uncle who had come over as a 49er and returned to Ireland a prosperous man.

James McAvoy never returned to Ireland. He must have fallen in love with the mountains or, perhaps, he spent his whole life believing he was on the verge of discovering a great treasure.

I know which treasure story it must have been to lure him to these mountains. It is the same treasure story that lures every prospector who comes here. It is the legend of the lost mine with the iron door. The legend dates back to the days of Spanish conquistadors and an old mission established by the Jesuits on the north side of the Santa Catalina Mountains, just beyond Tucson. The church was established among Native Americans whom the friars described as fierce. These Native Americans would come to be known as the Apache and the church was called *Santa Catalina de Cuitabaga* an Apache word meaning "spring" where the people gather mesquite beans. It later became known as the "lost mine with the iron door." This is how the story appeared in print in the *Arizona Weekly Star* of February 4, 1880.

"The principal gold mines were situated in these mountains. There was a place called Nueva Mia Ciudad, having a monster church with a number of golden bells that were used to summon the laborers from the fields and mines. It was a short distance from the city, which was situated on a plateau. It was a mine of such fabulous richness that the miners used to cut gold out with a 'hatcheta.'

"At the time of the Franciscans acquiring supremacy, the Jesuits fled, leaving the city destitute of population. Before their flight they placed an iron door on the mine and secured it in such a manner that it would require a considerable time to unfasten it. There were only two entrances to this city and they also were closed. All traces were obliterated so as to throw the Franciscans off the road to this Nueva Mia City."

It was quite a legend and a tremendous earthquake in the late 1800s created rumors that the Iron Door Mine had been buried beneath a massive avalanche. James McAvoy, the adventurous young man from Ireland, was not the only prospector to fall under the legend's spell.

The mountain pass, Charouleau Gap, is named after a

Swiss man who had lost the family fortune in Guatemala before searching for treasure in the Santa Catalinas. The town of Oracle was founded by prospectors and miners such as Alexander McKay. Harold Bell Wright wrote the novel *"The Mine with the Iron Door"* which became a movie in 1925.

McAvoy was known to be somewhat of a hermit, but from time to time he would leave his mine workings behind and venture into town to acquire supplies.

Oracle, like most frontier towns, had problems with stray dogs. In the days before spaying and neutering, canine populations frequently soared out of control. For a time, Tucson had a law which stated that, if a man saw a dog without a collar roaming the street and did not shoot it immediately, he could be arrested on the spot for not performing his civic duty.

James McAvoy would pull into Oracle for supplies and his first stop would be the local butcher shop. There McAvoy would purchase meat scraps and proceed to feed all the stray dogs in town. For the next few days, a pack of dogs would follow McAvoy wherever he went about town. He would toss them scraps from time to time. When his business had been transacted and it was time to leave town, McAvoy would make one last stop at the butcher shop. As the Irish prospector walked out of Oracle, all the stray dogs in town followed like he was the Pied Piper of Hamlin. The hungry dogs would follow him all the way to his remote mountain shack. It wasn't that McAvoy loved dogs, he saw himself as more of a rancher.

Weasel

chapter 24:
Juggling

On the outskirts of Las Vegas, flames leapt out from under the hood. The alternator was on fire. Flames jumped up a good two feet from the crevice where the hood lay against the frame.

Robert and I were on our way to Yosemite where a freak summer snowstorm had dumped 12 feet of snow on the high mountains.

First we had to visit Las Vegas. We had a plan for counting cards that we were certain would make us money playing blackjack, enough to pay for the backpacking trip and bring home a profit too. It was no problem buying an unexpected car part along the way.

We swapped out the alternator in the parking lot of the parts store and drove to the nearest casino. Our blackjack system failed miserably and we lost almost all our money at Circus Circus. We had just enough cash left for lunch and gas; not quite enough for gas but we would worry about that on the way home.

We ate lunch, watching the trapeze artists, eagerly anticipating Yosemite. Then we saw the most amazing thing.

There was this old guy wearing a flannel shirt, suspenders, and a flattop crew cut haircut. The old guy approached one of the Circus Circus clowns and whispered something in his ear. Next thing you know the clown handed over his balls, all three of them.

The guy in the suspenders began to juggle while the clown stood there and watched. It turned out the old guy was on vacation from Ringling Brothers and his wife had always wanted to see Vegas. While the old ordinary guy juggled, his little old lady wife stood behind him, beehive hairdo towering high.

One by one more and more clowns arrived, watching in amazement. More clowns gathered around to watch until 14 brightly colored clowns stood around the juggler. There were clowns with big shoes, oversized bow ties, red noses and frizzy green hair, watching every move of the most conservatively dressed man in Las Vegas with awe and wonder.

Hiking the high country in Yosemite, Robert and I got lost almost immediately. Snow markers on the trail are eight feet high, and the freak summer snow storm left twelve-foot-high drifts.

The hills were covered with a smooth, pristine blanket of white. The trees rose up in white-covered clumps and the granite mountains rose high above us, with little wisps of cloud clinging to the peaks like the last wisps of a bald man's hair.

We had no idea where the trail was but it is hard to feel lost when you are surrounded by so much beauty and splendor.

I knew I would like Tom as soon as I saw him. In the middle of all that snow, he was just as lost as we were. One look into his eyes and I could tell Tom was surrounded by beauty and splendor too. Plus, standing knee deep in the snow, he was hiking in shorts.

Since we were all lost, we decided to hike together. Tom had hitchhiked all the way to California from Massachusetts. He had a unique gimmick for catching rides. He would stand by the side of the road and juggle. When cars came by he would juggle with one hand and stick out a thumb on the other hand. It worked like a charm.

Juggling

We set up camp beside a roaring waterfall. There was a weasel living in the rock pile beside the tent. The long slender mammal was wearing his ermine white coat and we couldn't stop him from raiding our camp as he slithered in and out of rock crevices. Still, it was fun chasing him.

Tom, Robert, and I encircled the small hill of rocks while the weasel used his long slender body to wiggle in and out of tunnels. We would catch a glimpse of the weasel coming out at one spot. All three of us would descend with a great deal of whooping and hollering. Before the weasel's tail had completely exited one tunnel, the head was already entering the next doorway. He would slither away only to pop out somewhere else.

The weasel hung out around our campsite all night long, darting out from the shadows on the edge of the campfire to steal fallen dinner scraps, scampering away with his looted treasure, escaping deep inside the labyrinth of tunnels inside the small hill of rocks.

That night Tom began to juggle. Once in a while he dropped a ball. Tom told me it was important to drop the ball sometimes. He said he could blow through every trick he knew in about four minutes and it tended to leave people completely unimpressed because it looked too easy.

The idea was to start slowly, even drop the ball once in awhile, and then slowly build up to the harder tricks, ball over the shoulder, ball under the leg, take a bite from the apple, juggle four balls and so on until the tricks looked hard.

Tom began to tell me the true story of the John F. Kennedy assassination, juggling the whole time. He explained how LBJ and Richard Nixon were in on it together, and then Tom threw a ball over his shoulder. The conspiracy was tied to the rise of the Dallas Cowboys and the decline of the Boston Celtics. Tom replaced one of the juggling balls with an apple, lunged forward in mid circle and took a bite from the apple, still juggling.

William Randolph Hearst, the inspiration for *Citizen Kane* himself, was somehow involved in this conspiracy assassination theory. I can't remember exactly how because by that time Tom was juggling four balls at once. Suddenly he rifled a ball forward, the ball ricocheted off my forehead and returned to his palm, rejoining the circling rotation without interruption.

There in the Yosemite high country, Tom entertained me with one of the most amazing performances I have ever seen.

We sat around the campfire, drinking hot chocolate. Tom taught Robert how to juggle.

Eventually the clouds began to slowly cover the stars. This was bad. If it snowed again, no matter how slight, we might not be able to find our way out. Tom pointed out that as long as we remembered which way we had hiked in, there was no problem.

There in the darkness surrounding the campfire, we all pointed in the direction we thought would take us back to where the car was parked. Like foolish characters in a Three Stooges movie, we all pointed in different directions.

We awoke early in the morning and I discovered that, during the night, the weasel had climbed a tree, slithered out along a branch, and dropped down to raid my backpack. My backpack was filled apples, granola, pears, and oatmeal, but the only thing the weasel ate was my toothpaste. He consumed nearly an entire tube of toothpaste.

We ate a small breakfast, broke down camp and followed our footprints for two days until we got back to the car. Robert gave Tom a lift to the next trailhead and we started home.

Juggling

At a rest stop, halfway between Yuma and Gila Bend, Robert tried out his new juggling skills, entertaining an audience just long enough to raise a couple dollars to buy a few gallons of gas to get us home.

This all happened when I had just turned 18. To this day, it was one of the most incredible backpacking trips I have ever taken. I learned that you can be surrounded by beauty and splendor and still be lost, but it is not all that bad.

I learned that sometimes the biggest clown in the room looks the most ordinary. I learned that life is nothing if not a juggling act, especially politics and history.

Sometimes those ideas which stick with us are not the best ideas but they are those presented with the best showmanship. It does not hurt to drop the ball once in a while just to capture people's attention.

Most importantly, of all the woodland creatures in the forest, weasels have the prettiest teeth.

This illegal monument commemorates a standoff with law enforcement and suicide by dynamite and is hidden in the Santa Catalinas.

chapter 25:
Francis Mountain

I park my automobile at the big bend in Cody Loop Road. I open and close the cattle gate which marks the national forest boundary. I begin marching along the dirt road with a specific destination in mind. I am heading towards an illegal monument.

The trees are filled with avian chatter; cackling blue jays and others. There is one bird in particular that just won't shut up. Suddenly I spy a burst of red wings – a cardinal; one of the noisiest birds of the forest. When I turn from the main road and take the side road it gains elevation quickly. Trudging straight up the side of a hill, I lose my breath.

All that huffing and puffing frightens a deer from the underbrush. Other hikes have revealed javelina, bobcats, and foxes. The road continues to climb, not as steep but still gaining in elevation. My pulse quickens from the exertion as the road winds back and forth across the rugged Arizona mountain slopes.

The place I am headed to is not quite at the end of the road. The road dead ends at an old mine but that is not where the illegal monument is located. This monument, placed on government lands without government permission, is hidden off to the side in a little clump of bushes. If you didn't know where to look for it you might not see it. In the bushes is a small monument; maybe three feet tall adorned only with a brass plaque and hand-engraved letters. The plaque reads:

Earl Francis / August 15, 1966

His life ended on this mountain. He could not bear to see destroyed, by order of government personnel, his home, his faith in fellow man and all the things his flag stood for. His motto could well have been Live and Let Live. His life followed the Golden Rule. All found him loyal, generous, industrious, and self reliant. May his soul find tranquility in another place as beautiful as this.

Francis Mountain

The letters are not neatly stamped but one gets the feeling that the sentiments are genuine. The plaque is right about one thing – this is a beautiful place. It is a great place to go for sunsets when the Galiluro Mountains take on a crimson glow. From this peak I can see the San Manuel smelter and the bright colored rock of the Tiger Mine.

Earl Francis had been a miner, working the claims on the hill near the plaque. The federal government ruled that his mining claim was valid but it was illegal for him to reside here on forest service land. On August 15, 1966, Earl Francis strapped dynamite beneath his trailer and blew himself and his trailer to kingdom come before the government could haul either one away.

I pause to take a deep breath of mountain air. I light my pipe and take a puff of illicit freedom. There is something defiant about the Francis Mountain Monument. It reminds me of the monument just outside of Skeleton Canyon. That monument announces in proud bureaucratese that the surrender of Geronimo to General Crook at this spot, once upon a time, forever ended all forms of rebellion and resistance here in the great state of Arizona. The last time I visited the Skeleton Canyon Monument someone had scrawled graffiti in a felt pen in response. "BULLSHIT!" the graffiti proclaimed in a statement that was concise and an act of rebellion and resistance at the same time. The memory makes me smile.

I take another deep breath of fresh mountain air, another puff of illicit freedom, and pat the Francis Mountain Monument for good luck before I head back down the trail; racing the forces of darkness. I hike down whistling Yankee Doodle and feeling inspired to commit acts of mischievous virtue and random kindness.

chapter 26:
The Ballad of Pearl Hart

The last days of the wild west unofficially came to an end on May 29, 1899, when the Globe – Florence stagecoach was held up by a pair of bandits. This holdup was notable for two reasons. The first reason was that this was the very last stagecoach robbery in the history of the American west. The second reason this hold up was noteworthy is that one of the bandits was a woman – a woman named Pearl Hart.

Pearl Hart was born as Pearl Taylor in Lindsay, Ontario, Canada, in the year of 1878. After her career of infamy, a school chum wrote to the Arizona Historical Society and described the teenage girl he had known years before.

"She was a pretty girl and had a wonderful figure and voice; could imitate a croaking frog, an owl, a hawk, could sing like a mockingbird ... was lithesome, blithe and witty; gushing with fun and jollity; also a wonderful dancer, and very attractive. Everybody admired her and was proud of her acquaintance; but she possessed one detrimental fault which brought her many troubles. She was too amorous; accepted too many dates with handsome young men, which finally caused her undoing."

That undoing began in the shape of a young man named William Hart who married Pearl when she was just 16. William Hart was not willing to work except to earn just enough to slake his thirst for alcohol. Rather than starve, Pearl Hart hopped a train south of the border and eventually ended up in Phoenix, Arizona.

While a resident of Phoenix, she made the acquaintance of a dance-hall musician and tin-horn gambler named Dan Bandman. Bandman taught Pearl how to drink, smoke, and even how to use opium. Their relationship was interrupted when Dan enlisted into the Spanish American War.

For awhile, Pearl made her living in Mammoth, Arizona, cooking for miners in a tent pitched along the shores of the San Pedro River. Soon she made her way north to Globe, Arizona. It was while in Globe that she met her future partner in crime, a German named Joe Boot. When Dan Bandman appeared on the scene asking for money, Joe Boot helped Pearl drive her former lover away. Together, Joe and Pearl worked a small mining claim. Unfortunately the ore was worthless. One day, a letter arrived from back east announcing that Pearl's mother was gravely ill and that if Pearl wished one last visit she had better hightail it home soon. Pearl and Joe came up with a desperate plan.

On that infamous day, Henry Bacon was sitting atop the stagecoach as the driver. He had a Colt .45 revolver on him but it was not loaded as he did not expect to use it. The days of Indian raids and stagecoach robberies were long gone. In fact, the Florence – Globe line was one of the few stagecoach lines that had not yet been replaced by the railroad. There were three passengers enduring the jolts of the rugged mountain road – a traveling salesman, a tenderfoot "with his hair parted in the middle" and a Chinaman. As the driver approached the sharp turn at Cane Springs, he applied the brakes to slow down. As he did so, two unmasked bandits leapt from the bushes – both holding weapons.

The driver stopped and the passengers exited. Although dressed as a man it was obvious by the swell of her bosom that the smaller of the two thieves was a woman. While Joe Boot held a shotgun on the stagecoach passengers, Pearl searched the victims and put the money in a burlap sack. The salesman was carrying $380 dollars in cash, the tenderfoot $36, and the Chinaman $5. The bandits took it all plus the salesman's watch. As they prepared to leave Pearl returned a dollar to each man, providing "just enough to eat."

Pinal County Sheriff W. E. Truman was soon hot on the

desperadoes' trail and traced them to a schoolhouse 20 miles north of Benson. The posse snuck up on the dangerous duo while they were sleeping. A newspaper named *The Silver Belt* described their capture. "The officers came up, removed their armament and awoke them. The woman sprang up, fighting, but the man made no resistance. His companion reproached him in vile and profane language and said that if the posse had tried to capture her while she was awake, she would have made some holes in it."

While in jail Pearl became an instant celebrity. Again, the Silver Belt described the scene: "The woman is receiving much attention, an afternoon rarely going by without her having lots of callers and herself being photographed. The camera fiends have taken shots of her with all sorts of firearms and looking as much the desperado as they can make her."

The commotion in Florence was too much for Sheriff Truman to handle and soon Ms. Hart was shipped to the Pima County Jail in Tucson. A man named Ed Hogan, a notorious bicycle thief who was serving a sentence for being drunk and disorderly, quickly befriended Pearl. Hogan had nearly finished his sentence and was a trusty at the jail. He fell in love with the female bandit and she enlisted his aid in her escape. At night, Ed Hogan cut a hole in Pearl's plaster wall and she had escaped, but not before leaving behind a note which declared her a fan of the campaign for woman's emancipation.

An editorial writer for the *Arizona Star* was impressed with her arguments. He wrote, "That laws should be enacted by the consent of the governed is a fundamental principle of our government ... Woman is not given the right to consent to the enactment of the laws which provide these penalties. Then why should she be made to suffer."

The big city newspapers back east soon made the Lady Bandit a celebrity and a bit of a Robin-Hood-type hero. Arizona newspapers and the law enforcement figures who had been forced to deal with her replied that many of her troubles were of her own making and even her own family was forced to admit publicly that Pearl was quite an opium fiend. Pearl Hart and Ed Hogan ran off to Deming, New Mexico, where she attempted to set herself up as a sort of queen of thieves. She was soon recaptured.

On June 15, 1899, Pear Hart and Joe Boot came up for trial. Joe pleaded guilty and was sentenced to 35 years in jail. Despite the hundreds of times Pearl had not only admitted and even boasted of her part in the crime, Pearl chose this moment to plead her innocence. The jury came back with a verdict of not guilty. Judge F. M. Dean was outraged by this verdict and had the bailiff immediately arrest Pearl Hart. He roasted the jury for their dereliction of duty. Pearl was immediately tried again on the charge of stealing the stagecoach driver's pistol. This time the jury gave her five years in prison.

She was sent to the Territorial Prison in Yuma. It was said that on her journey to her new residence she puffed cigars constantly, emitting a stream of smoke which matched that of the locomotive in which she was riding.

The celebrity circus continued. The guards lost interest in watching the other prisoners and gravitated towards her cell with a hilarious enthusiasm that was harmful to discipline. There were also visiting newspapermen and the camera fiends who always begged the warden to let her pose in the jail yard with a six shooter or a Winchester. On December 19, 1902, two years before her sentence was up, Pearl Hart was pardoned by Territorial Governor Brodie. The governor explained the pardon by stating that the Yuma Prison lacked accommodations for women prisoners. Nearly half a century later historian Bert Fireman uncovered the true story for the *Arizona Republic*. Pearl Hart was pardoned when the prison doctor confirmed that the female prisoner was pregnant. Rather than allow the scandal of a baby being both conceived and born in prison, Pearl Hart was pardoned on the governor's sole condition that she leave Arizona for good.

After her release from prison Pearl Hart disappears from certainty in the historical record. Some claim that she appeared on the vaudeville stage in a play about her exploits as the lady bandit in a show bankrolled by William Randolph Hearst. Others state that she may have briefly appeared in the Buffalo Bill Wild West Show. There were rumors that she ran a gang of pickpockets in Kansas City, while others place her in this fine metropolis but believe she only ran a cigar store while there. There was even one anecdote about a tour guide leading a group through the old Pima County Jail. At the end of the tour a little old lady came up and confessed, "Thanks for showing me where I stayed for awhile. I'm Pearl Hart." Then she walked away.

The last theories about Pearl Hart's whereabouts come from some old time Arizona pioneers who believe that she settled down as a rancher's wife on a homestead outside Globe, not far from Cane Springs and the site of the stagecoach robbery which provided her moment of celebrity infamy. The woman who some believe might have been Pearl Hart passed away on December 30, 1955.

chapter 27:
Gunfight at the Tunnel Saloon

On May 31, 1888, former deputy Josephus Phy stood outside the Tunnel Saloon, on the sidewalks of Florence, Arizona, and waited with a loaded revolver in one hand and a Bowie knife in the other. The intended object of his anger, former sheriff Peter Gabriel sat at the bar in the Tunnel Saloon, sipping suds and shooting the breeze. Gabriel seemed in no hurry to leave. Impatient, Phy charged inside the saloon doors and the infamous gunfight began. By the time the deadly battle ended, it had spilled into the streets of Florence and left one man dead and two others badly wounded.

Back in the days when Florence was a rowdy frontier town, the favorite watering hole of cowboys, homesteaders, outlaws, and lawmen was the Tunnel Saloon. It earned the name because the entire establishment had been built underground. The cool cavernous temperature was a delight to one and all in the hot summer months long before air conditioning had been invented. The Tunnel Saloon used to be located in the heart of downtown Florence. It was where Dick's Pool Hall now stands.

I first learned of the infamous gunfight at the Tunnel Saloon while I was visiting Florence on a warm afternoon. I stopped in a modern establishment named My Office Bar. One wall inside the tavern is adorned with a beautiful mural; an artist's rendition of the gunfight at the Tunnel Saloon. Inspired by the beautiful painting I became curious about the sequence of events that transpired that bloody afternoon.

Inquiring of the locals inside My Office Bar, I was quickly given three slightly different and vague versions of the historic events. It was late in the day and I needed to be headed home but I resolved right then and there to return to Florence and unearth the story of the gunfight at the Tunnel Saloon.

Sheriff Peter Gabriel was born in Prussia in 1838 and migrated to the American West where he immediately began a career in the violent frontier profession of law enforcement. Gabriel hired on as a deputy sheriff in Los Angeles and then as a lawman in Idaho. In California, Gabriel received a shotgun blast to the chest and had a hole so large that a grapefruit could have been placed inside it. One lung collapsed. Gabriel recovered and eventually moved to Arizona where he secured a job in Wickenburg, riding shotgun on the stagecoaches.

During his stay in Wickenburg Gabriel became involved in a deadly confrontation. Peter Gabriel loved to gamble while playing cards and it was during one of these "friendly" card games that Gabriel accused another man of cheating. The accused man drew a knife and began to lunge across the table. Gabriel drew his revolver and shot the man in the heart, killing him instantly. A jury found Gabriel innocent on account of self defense.

Peter Gabriel became the first elected sheriff of Pinal County in 1878. Soon legends began to spread about his prowess with fire arms. Some of the accounts listed by J. A. Swearengin in his book *Good Men, Bad Men, Law Men* and a few rowdy ladies, include the claim that Gabriel could shoot while seated in a rolling wagon and hit jackrabbitts running in the brush. There is another story where he is credited with shooting a kidnapper as he rode past at full gallop. Not only did a single bullet from Gabriel's revolver drop the bandit dead but it left the beautiful young lady in his arms unharmed. The girl was returned to her parents and Gabriel's legend spread.

A Florence citizen named Paisano was riding into the local saloons on horseback, riding his steed all the way up to the bar. He removed his revolver from the holster before ordering the bartender to pour a round of drinks for the house. Paisano and his horse went from bar to bar and had held up almost every saloon when Gabriel caught up with him. As Gabriel approached the saloon, Paisano and his horse emerged, riding away. Gabriel ordered Paisano to halt and the generous bandit only spurred his horse to go faster. Gabriel's single shot passed through Paisano and went into the horse's head, killing both instantly.

It was Gabriel who brought Josephus Phy to Florence, luring him with the offer of a job as a deputy. Josephus Phy had a reputation as a terror to criminals. When he went after an outlaw, they generally came down. Phy was ambidextrous and deadly with either hand. Deputy Phy liked to head into battle with a Bowie knife in one hand and a revolver in the other, shifting them back and forth.

Gabriel fired his deputy after it was claimed that Phy had unnecessarily beaten a man in Casa Grande. This forced Gabriel to evict Phy from his living quarters above the county jail. While moving out, Phy loaded many of his belongings into a black leather satchel belonging to Gabriel. The tension in the feud escalated even more during the next election when Gabriel retired as sheriff but threw his recommendation behind another candidate for the post, Jere Fryer. Phy felt Gabriel's support had been promised to him.

As always though, the root of the true bitterness between the two men was over the heart of a beautiful woman. Peter Gabriel had a beautiful wife who bore him three children. Mrs. Gabriel was also half her husband's age and, as is often the case in June/ December marriages, the husband was a jealous man. His anger boiled whenever any other man received a moment of her attention or one of her sunbeam smiles. Tired of what she perceived as unreasonable jealousy, the married couple separated and lived apart. Ex-deputy Phy became her protector about town.

The Arizona Historical Society has on record a quote by local Florence resident Michael Rice describing a time when he saved Phy's life. "One day as Gabriel and myself were sitting in sheriff Fryer's office chatting, we saw Joe Phy standing diagonally across the street about 200 feet away. Presently, Gabriel's little daughter approached Phy and handed him a note. Phy took the piece of paper and commenced to read it. Gabriel, observing the act, jumped to his feet and grasping a rifle close to hand, raised it to fire. I grasped his arm and bore down on the weapon, before he could draw a bead on the object of his insane jealousy. Phy stepped out of sight around the corner and unknowingly avoided what would have been instant death. Gabriel started to follow his intended victim, but I persuaded him to desist. For once he listened to reason and placed the Winchester against the desk. The note given to Phy by the little girl proved to be an order on the Rittenhouse Store for groceries, with a request they be brought to the home."

A final incident escalated the bad blood to the boiling point. Phy and Gabriel met in the town of Casa Grande one day and a verbal confrontation followed. The harsh words quickly led to a fist fight right in the middle of a Casa Grande street. Gabriel won this battle and arrested Phy, hauling him into the Florence jail and humiliating him. Phy's anger had reached the point of no return and he began to boast of his upcoming revenge. Once, while cooling off in the Tunnel Saloon, Phy stood two silver dollars on edge before slicing through them with his Bowie knife and announcing that he was about to do the same to Gabriel.

The feud was settled on May 31, 1888, with the bloody encounter which has come to be known as the gunfight at the Tunnel Saloon. There are several different versions of what happened next. One reason for this is that the first shots blew out all the lights in the tavern. The part we know for sure is that Peter Gabriel had made a trip into town from the mine he was operating in the Dripping Springs Mountains and was kicking back his heels and enjoying a drink at the Tunnel Saloon. Gabriel had been forewarned that Phy was waiting for him outside. The veteran lawman knew that, when he stepped outside from the dark underground tavern, he would be temporarily blinded.

On my return to Florence, I made my first stop at the Chamber of Commerce building which is decorated in the baroque-Victorian, architectural style which was all the rage back when Florence was being built. The nice lady inside recommended that I head down the street to Taylor's Bed and Breakfast where the proprietor was well acquainted with the history of the gunfight. Mr. Taylor was enthused to share his historical expertise with us. In the lobby of his bed and breakfast was a framed document which gave a brief background of the gunfight and the aftermath. There was one thing the document did not tell. He explained, "When Josephus Phy entered the saloon he spied Gabriel and fired. The bullet went right through Gabriel's heart. The only problem was that Phy had just shot Gabriel's reflection in the mirror. This gave the former sheriff a chance to turn and shoot, striking Phy. The two men continued shooting and the gunfight spilled onto the Florence sidewalks. Gabriel shot Phy four times and Phy returned the favor three times. Gabriel had gained the advantage from the mistaken shot into the mirror." Taylor had another surprise. The Tunnel Saloon mirror, with the bullet hole, was in storage at his bed and breakfast. I inspected the mirror and tried to imagine the volatile scene that day.

An eyewitness account at the coroner's inquest, by one of the owners of the Tunnel Saloon, Captain Jack Keating, claimed that he was certain it was Gabriel who fired first although Phy did enter the door with his six-shooter drawn.

Another witness, Peter R. Brady, claimed that the first two shots were fired so close together that they could not have both come from the gun of one man.

Although there is some question as to the beginning of the fight, there is no doubt as to the aftermath. The first gun shots blew out all the lights and the two combatants fired until Gabriel had been hit three times and Phy four. Wounded, Phy fell backwards out into the street. Gabriel, bleeding profusely, got up and walked calmly from the bar, stepping over his assailant on his way, until he collapsed in front of the OK Livery Stable.

The bartender, a man named Gibson rushed to aid Phy. There had been some previous bad blood between the two men and, although Phy had dropped his pistol, he still held the Bowie knife in his left hand. He plunged the blade into the bartender's thigh. It was a deep flesh wound but the bartender would eventually recover.

Messengers ran to fetch Dr. Harvey who came almost immediately. The good doctor reached the fallen Phy first but there was nothing he could do to aid the wounded man. Phy died shortly after midnight. When the doctor came to Gabriel's aid, Peter refused his help because the doctor had checked Phy first and therefore, in the mind of Gabriel at least, the doctor had chosen sides. Gabriel waited 12 hours until the doctor from Sacaton on the reservation could arrive. Even though one of the bullets passed through his remaining good lung, Gabriel survived quite nicely.

I ended my journey back where it all began, on a bar stool at My Office Bar, gazing upon the beautiful mural which depicts the gunfight at the Tunnel Saloon. I was explaining to one of the patrons about the mirror with the bullet hole when he exclaimed, "Why it didn't happen that way at all. We have a pane of glass in the historical society from the Tunnel

Saloon gunfight, from when the battle spilled into the street."

All I could do was chuckle, even more than a century later the gunfight still drew excited partisan support from local residents. I learned that sometimes research does not clear up the foggy clouds of history but only leads to more detailed questions. As I pondered these thoughts, a new customer bellied up to the bar and ignored the beautiful mural. Instead, his attention was riveted by the wall of stuffed and mounted animal heads which are displayed behind the bar. He pointed to species of beast that he did not recognize.

"What is that?" he asked.

"I don't know," the bartender answered, "But it sure was running fast when it crashed through that wall."

Sheriff Peter Gabriel as depicted in a Florence mural

chapter 28:
A Handful of Arizona Christmases

William F. Cody, metal cutout by Jerry Parra

The honored guest stood beside the Christmas tree and spoke to the audience in a foreign language. The children looked on with confused wonder. William F. Cody made a fine Santa Claus. He already had the long white hair and the white beard. Cody spoke in kind tones but used words from a strange tongue. Cody greeted his audience in the Sioux language, telling of the Sioux conception of the Great Spirit and how the Great Spirit had sent Santa Claus to earth to gladden the hearts of all the children in the world. The audience cheered.

It was the winter of 1912 and Oracle was experiencing their most famous Christmas. Cody had been an army scout and explorer for many years, but it was as an actor and promoter for his Wild West Shows that he gained international fame. Cody had only recently moved to the Oracle area, investing in Campo Bonito and the High Jinks Mine. His acting career had been on the decline recently and Cody just knew that, if he could make enough money at the High Jinks, he could reinvest in his thespian pursuits. There was a newfangled technology called motion pictures. Cody just knew that if he could somehow combine his wild-west shows with this new technology he would have a sure-fire hit.

When asked to perform as Santa Claus for the children of Oracle, Cody quickly agreed. Families came on horseback, burro, and wagon to see the show. Cody arrived by automobile and for many of the people in attendance it was the first car they had ever seen. Not only did the children get to see Santa Claus but Buffalo Bill was one of the most famous celebrities on the planet. Cody was charming; dancing with each and every lady, waltzing up and down the dance floor. Cody's ranch hands presented him with a jaguar pelt. The ferocious feline had been trapped in Campo Bonito and was the last jaguar legally taken in Arizona. In her book *Paradise Found*, Kathy Alexander describes the merry Christmas, "After the many gifts had been dispensed, sports were in order and the balance of the afternoon was taken up in foot races for the little boys and girls, in burro races, shooting matches, etc . . . Colonel Cody has won fame in many lines but the little children of the Catalina Mountains will always remember him as a dear old Santa who gave them lots of toys."

In Arizona, *Christmas* is not just a holiday but a place. The town of Christmas is located nine miles north of Winkleman, high on the cliffs above the Gila River. Christmas is now a ghost town, but in the spring the steep slopes are covered with beautiful orange poppies; a clue to the copper hidden beneath the soil. Christmas had an earlier history and previous names. Mining operations were opened in 1878 and 1882 only to be shut down when it was discovered they were occupying reservation lands. The rich copper deposits were left undisturbed until 1902 when N. J. Mellon and George Crittenden realized that a recent redrawing of reservation boundaries had excluded the area from Apache lands. The two men rushed in, naming both the town and the mine after the day they arrived.

Three months later, the post office officially christened the town Christmas, Arizona. The official historical dates of western ghost towns are usually designated by the opening and closing of the U. S. Post Office. The Christmas post office was closed on March 30, 1935, officially making Christmas a ghost town.

They say that the largest ruins left in Christmas are of the general store which used to have the post-office window inside. During the holiday season, it became the most important place in town as thousands and thousands of parcels, cards, letters, and packages came through the little town to get the distinctive Christmas postmark.

The biggest year-around industry in town was copper mining. Located in the Dripping Springs Mountains, Christmas sat on a huge ore deposit. During its heyday the industry supported as many as 1,000 residents. From time to time, the ownership of the town changes hands. The claims are still occasionally worked and sometimes temporary residents move to Christmas and live alongside the ghosts of past prospectors and, perhaps, a few elves.

Arizona is also the home of a Christmas tragedy. Santa Claus was killed in Mesa in 1932. This tragic event took place during the Great Depression. The horrific occasion was witnessed by hundreds. Traumatized children broke into uncontrollable sobbing and the tears fell like waterfalls.

In 1932, the Great Depression had cast dark economic clouds across the nation. Mesa was hit hard by financial woes. It looked as if the annual Christmas parade would have to be cancelled. The colorful editor of the *Mesa Tribune*, John McPhee, came up with a flamboyant promotional scheme to save the Christmas parade.

McPhee wanted to begin the parade beside an open field on the outskirts of town. A small plane would circle overhead and Santa Claus would skydive, arriving not by reindeer-drawn sled but floating down from the heavens beneath a billowing white canopy. Once he had landed in the open field Santa would unharness the parachute to thunderous applause before triumphantly leading the Christmas parade.

Merchants, wounded by dismal financial times, were

willing to back any plan that might boost lagging Christmas sales. A small plane was rented and a stunt man was found who agreed to undertake the daredevil act, leaping from an airplane armed with only a Santa Claus suit and a parachute.

The morning of the big event, shortly before the parade itself, Santa was nowhere to be found. An anxious McPhee paced and stalled, sending people everywhere in search of the fugitive Santa. It was one of the elves who discovered Santa plastered to a bar stool in a local tavern trying to drink up some courage. The wayward Santa Claus was too intoxicated to stand. Determined not to cancel the flamboyant beginning of the heavily promoted Christmas extravaganza, McPhee asked the local merchants for volunteers to make the Santa jump. There were no takers. McPhee himself found the task a little too daunting.

Desperate times forced a desperate plan. McPhee put the Santa Claus suit on a department-store dummy. The mannequin would be pushed from the airplane and float down into the field. McPhee, wearing a second Santa Claus suit would be hiding in the tall grass and leap out where the mannequin had landed, greet the crowd and quickly start the Christmas parade before anyone could ask questions.

The moment arrived. A sizable crowd gathered on the edge of the field, waiting anxiously, when the sputtering of the approaching aircraft could be heard. Squinting into the sun, the people cheered when the tiny airplane carrying Santa Claus could first be seen. The pilot circled low above the crowd, hovering so close above the heads of the astonished spectators that they were able to see the department store dummy wearing the red suit standing in the doorway, his white beard flapping in the breeze. The plane ascended in a gradual spiral and, at its peak, the mannequin Santa was pushed from the doorway. The static line pulled but the chute failed to open. Santa fell from the sky, dropping, dropping, dropping to the earth in a red and white blur. He plummeted, white beard, red cap, and tangled chute waving wildly behind him. Children screamed. Santa landed in the field with a horrific splat. Women fainted.

Without the open parachute to create a wind drift, the pilot had miscalculated where the mannequin would land. By the time McPhee had run to where Santa crashed most of the crowd were trying to comfort their sobbing children. McPhee leapt over the mangled Santa and went "Ta-Da" but no one was watching.

William Cody wall as depicted at Sue & Jerry's Ranch Store Center in Oracle

The parade went on as scheduled but most of the crowd went home before it even started. Those few who remained were quiet. It almost seemed like more of a funeral procession than a parade. McPhee spent most of the next few weeks laying low. Christmas sales did not improve. McPhee continued a long career as a civic leader until his death 40 years later. The headline of his obituary could not help but mention the demise "of the man who killed Santa Claus."

Last year the *Arizona Republic* obituaries column reported the demise of a gentleman who had taken part in the Christmas Truce of World War I. On Christmas morning in 1914, the eerie sound of silence enveloped the Western Front. For months the battlefield trenches had been filled with awful noises such as the hissing, cracking, and whining of bullets in flight. There was the mechanical scream of rapid-fire machine guns. There were distant voices in French, German, and English. These voices were cursing, praying, moaning and crying. The roar of the artillery was deafening: Boom, boom, scream, death, boom.

The morning of December 25th, 1914, there was nothing but quiet; silence as far as the ear could hear. Someone shouted, "Merry Christmas" even though no one was merry. The joy spread as if it were contagious. Soldiers emerged from their trenches, exchanged cigarettes and photographs. They played soccer amidst the mud and barbed wire making sure that men from all nations were represented on both teams. They stood arm in arm and sang Christmas carols in each of their languages.

The generals were alarmed, afraid that spontaneous fraternization would sap the will of the infantry to fight. They ordered the artillery fired, ending the beautiful eerie silence, so the killing could start again. Before the war was done, five more years and ten million lives were gone. The spontaneous Christmas truce was never repeated. It was a short peace hidden inside a terrible war.

chapter 29:
The Aviator's Ghost

I walk along this forest path for the first time in many years and I try to fight back the fear. It is a silly feeling, the remnants of childhood superstitions running through my veins. It is a beautiful day in one of the most glorious parts of the forest atop the Santa Catalina Mountains. Yet my eyes search the shadows for danger. The wind flutters the aspen leaves and suddenly there is a shriek in the forest canopy. I stop dead in my tracks and wheel around, just in time to see a blue-feathered jay fly from one tree to another. I take a deep breath and try to calm my nerves, feeling foolish for being afraid of a story I heard as a child.

Still, no matter what the logical parts of my brain try to tell me, my bones remember. I can dimly recall being a small child and camping in these very same mountains with family and friends. At night we would gather around the campfire and roast marshmallows. As the dusk stretched towards midnight and I began to drift towards sleep it would become time for storytelling. Mostly, there were tall tales and cowboy jokes. Last, as the embers of the fire were dying down, would come the ghost stories.

Usually the ghost stories were everybody's favorite part of the evening. Everybody's but mine. Even at a young age I found most of the ghost stories to be too exaggerated to be scary and discovered many of them to be downright silly. All of the stories except one failed to scare me. There was one campfire ghost story which always held my attention, one campfire story that not only scared me but haunted my nightmares.

The story is known as *The Aviator's Ghost*. It is not some transplanted recycled legend but a local piece of Tucson folklore. In fact, I am not sure if the story ever spread beyond my immediate family and my parents' friends. What I do

157

remember for certain is the feeling of being a wide-eyed little boy listening carefully to every word of *The Aviator's Ghost*.

For one thing, I had visited the scene of the crime. That is what I am doing this day, hiking to a place where I was taken as a boy. I just need to see for myself if viewing this place as an adult measures up to my memories of what I saw as a child. Today, however, just setting foot on the old trail has sent chills up and down my spine.

The trail is the Butterfly Loop, located about three-quarters of the way up the Santa Catalinas. It is a beautiful part of the mountain, located on the north slopes and is one of the greenest parts of the range. The trail winds along the ridge, passing turnoffs for Crystal and Novio Springs. I am headed to neither of those places.

My destination is a deep bend in the mountain just after Novio Springs where the water trickles over the rocks in a small fall. The canyon holds one of the thickest stands of sycamore trees in the Tucson area and is well worth the long hike to see the autumn leaves change colors. The forest floor is carpeted with the red and gold leaves from previous autumns. Scattered among the brightly colored leaves are the ruins of an airplane wreck. That is why I am here.

Deep in the heart of the Butterfly Loop are the ruins of an airplane, the remnants of the wreck that left behind the aviator's ghost. Shiny metal pieces lie just far enough off the trail so they can't be easily seen. There are scattered chunks of wing, engine, fuselage and tail strewn about the forest floor. These metal pieces no longer lie in an assembled path but are slowly sliding down the slope, becoming half buried in the gold and rust colored leaves. The plane is old and from the 1950s. The way many of the pieces are half buried in the forest belies the age of the wreck.

When the search and rescue teams raced to the plane

wreck, following the flames and the smell of destruction, they were not able to find most of the pilot. The search party did find the aviator's legs in the cockpit but they never discovered what happened to the rest of him. Thus began the legend of the ghost of a legless aviator traveling the mountain slopes of the Santa Catalinas.

Our parents took us to this place and showed us the airplane wreck like a sacred shrine. We were told this story so we might learn a valuable lesson. Be careful, our parents would warn us, of where we placed our things like jackets, hats, and lunches. It was important not to lose things in the forest while hiking. Items left unattended, especially food, had a way of disappearing; especially if the ghost of the legless aviator needed supplies. In fact, sometimes when he was really hungry, Stumpy the Pilot would devour lost little boys and girls who hadn't listened to their parents.

As a child I used to have nightmares about the aviator's ghost running wild on the slopes of the Santa Catalinas. Legless, the aviator's ghost no doubt preferred the forest canopy swinging from branch to branch, tree to tree. The nightmare which visited and revisited me time and again in my childhood involved being chased. In the dream I was little, five or six, and lost, wandering in the forest. Suddenly there was the sound of drums and a rustling atop the branches of some impossibly tall trees. A Tarzan-like yodel interrupted the forest stillness and Stumpy the Pilot emerged from the forest canopy, hunting me down as he swung from vine to vine. I ran as fast as my little legs would carry me, breaking into the open country of the grasslands. The ghost of the legless aviator dropped from the trees and swung from his knuckles, propelling himself by using his powerful muscular shoulders as a giant pendulum. He sprinted through the tall grass, nearly as high as the crown of his aviator's cap and mirror sunglasses, as fast as any cheetah streaking down prey in the savanna. I would wake up screaming.

When my mother came to the door to ask what was the matter I would lie and tell her nothing. I was afraid that, if I revealed my nightmares, we would stop hiking to the airplane wreck. It was my favorite spot on the mountain. We used to call the plane wreck Stumpy's House and always paid our respects with solemn silence. I hope his ghost haunts these mountain slopes forever. Towards that end, we intend to take my nephew, Joshua, hiking there this autumn and show him where the ghost of the legless aviator lives. I hope he has nightmares.

chapter 30:
The Camel's Gold

On November 28, 1913, the *Tucson Star* carried a story about a man from Ajo named John Nelson who reported seeing three camels in the desert. Nelson and his horse pursued the three beasts but the camels quickly outraced the horse across the desert sands. Skeptics questioned the story because it was first told in a saloon but, generally speaking, Nelson's tale is considered the last reliable sighting of a wild camel in Arizona.

The camel-cavalry experiment was begun on May 14, 1856, in Indianola, Texas. The camels had made a long journey from Egypt across the Atlantic Ocean to Texas. Four camels had died during the voyage but six more were born on ship. It was the beginning of the U.S. Army's camel cavalry, a short lived adventure that was quickly terminated by the Civil War.

I was surprised when my friend and rogue companion, Banjo Burch, began to talk to me about wild camels in the Arizona desert. Like Nelson's story it was first told over a few beers in a tavern. Banjo told me that he had been observing some most unusual hoof prints in the mountains near his ranch. They did not belong to horses or cattle and were far too large to belong to javelina or bighorn sheep. He was hopeful that the tracks might belong to the last surviving wild camel.

There was a famous treasure story he told me, about a lost prospector following a camel to a water hole. The water hole saved the prospector's life. When his thirst was satisfied he noticed that the sand at the bottom of the water hole was filled with gold dust.

He took as much gold dust as he could fit inside his pocket

and managed to find his way back to civilization. The gold assayed out to a nice value but the prospector was never able to find the gold-lined water hole again.

This treasure story is only one of many colorful anecdotes associated with the Arizona camels. The Arizona camel story really begins that day back in Indianola, Texas, when the camels were unloaded off the boats onto the docks. Lieutenant David O. Porter described it:

"The animals, led by their American and Oriental guides, marched down the gangplank in a most docile manner. The moment they hit solid earth however, their docile manner changed. They became excited and uncontrollable. They reared, kicked, cried, broke their halters, tore up their picket lines, and engaged in other fantastic tricks such as pawing and biting each other. The Texans, at first amused by these antics, became panic stricken and fled."

The camel caravan had been approved by President Franklin Pierce and was the pet project of Secretary of War Jefferson Davis. Davis would gain greater fame in his later job as President of the Confederacy during the Civil War. Lieutenant Edward F. Beale led the camel caravan on their first expedition, a topographical survey from Texas to California.

Beale was quick to praise the camels in his letters to Jefferson Davis. The camels were swift across the open desert sands, carried loads of up to 600 pounds, and they could go days without water. Their numbers quickly swelled from what one enlisted man described as "a loud and vigorous breeding program." The ships of the desert in the Sahara sailed smoothly in the Sonoran Desert as well.

There were problems however. The camels only seemed to respond to Arabic swear words. American muleskinners did not quite have the touch. Several of the middle-eastern camel jockeys would go on to become legendary heroes of the southwest. Most of them such as Hadji Ali and George Xaralampo became famous through their nicknames of Hi Jolly and Greek George. One frustrated American muleskinner described the camels as ornery, obstinate, stubborn and incorrigible. Those were only the printable words. There were also frequent complaints about the peculiar and potent body odor of the camels which tended to frighten other domesticated animals such as horses, dogs, and cattle.

When the camel cavalry experiment was abandoned by the army some of the beasts were sold to circuses, others to eccentric farmers, and some were simply set free to run wild across the desert. The feral camels did quite well. If the Nelson story can be considered reliable the camels survived for three quarters of a century in the Arizona desert. If my friend Banjo Burch has correctly identified the mysterious hoof prints out on the land near his ranch then perhaps there are still a few remaining wild camels roaming the rugged, remote mountains of Arizona.

The camels had no known natural predators in Arizona except for mankind. In his book *The Gila*, Edwin Corle recounts a capture of wild camels by the Pimas as described by a Prescott newspaper in December 30, 1881:

"A capture of camels has been made by Indians in the vicinity of Gila Bend and last Wednesday a carload passed by on their way to the east. While they stopped at the depot quite a large crowd gathered to see them. The carload consisted of seven large and two small ones and were consigned to a circus menagerie at Kansas City. They were in the charge of an Egyptian, Al Zel, who had been sent out expressly to get them. They do not differ from ordinary camels seen in this country except that they exceed in size any ever yet exhibited. The price said to be paid for them is trifling, the Indians being very anxious to be rid of them as their horses and

cattle are greatly frightened by them. There are still a large number in that vicinity."

As the camels grew rarer and rarer the stories surrounding them grew taller and taller. The most persistent of these rumors involved a large, white, male camel and his harem of brides. Hadji Ali is said to have met his death because of the white camel.

The popular camel driver, more commonly known as Hi Jolly, traded in his camel saddle for a prospector's pick and shovel. He was one of the first prominent settlers of the town of Quartszite, Arizona. There is a historical plaque erected in his honor. The tale of Hi Jolly's death, like many of the camel stories, involves a saloon. Hi Jolly was sitting at the bar waiting out a rare blizzard high in the mountains when a grizzled prospector staggered in claiming to have seen a herd of camels led by a large white male, half buried in a snow drift. Homesick for his native land and lonely for the ornery beasts he loved so much, Hadji Ali marched into the snow to rescue the camels. He froze to death.

"To the camel treasure," my friend Banjo Burch declared, raising his beer mug in a toast. "I have my shovel and my gold pan in the back of my pickup truck and I am going to go out treasure hunting this weekend."

"To the camel treasure," I say and clink glasses.

"You are always in the library," Banjo asserts, "See if you can look up the story of the lost camel treasure for me."

So I spent some time in the library and discovered the story of the lost camel's gold but I have some bad news for my friend. The lost treasure does not take place in the mountains near his house. According to Bill Broyles the tale goes like this:

Two adventurers, a Mexican named Juan Perea and a

Scotsman named John Gordon, were prospecting in the mountains along the Colorado River. They scrambled and searched for gold in the Trigo Mountains, the Chocolates, the Castle Domes, and the Kofas, before stumbling into the Tank Mountains. They explored the Tank Mountains for nearly a month, living off pork and beans and whatever water they could dip from canyon potholes.

They had no luck finding gold. Soon they were having no luck finding water. Thirst became a problem and then a danger in the dry, arid desert. One afternoon the two thirsty prospectors slept, hiding from the sun, joking about their impending doom. They were awakened by a camel traversing the rocky canyon floor, heading deep into the mountain. Camels are creatures of the open desert; their feet are easily cut open by craggy canyon floors. The two prospectors knew that there was only one reason a camel would travel this deep into a mountain and that was water. They were saved!

Perea and Gordon followed the camel to a narrow crevice still half full of water from the spring rains. The camel drank its fill, the prospectors slaked their thirst and relaxed, savoring their good fortune. Then the miners noticed that the pool's sandy bottom was lined with gold nuggets. Perea and Gordon filled their pockets with treasure and topped off their canteens with even more precious water before returning to civilization.

The miners spent all their gold outfitting an expedition to return to the Tank Mountains, laden with supplies and intending to work the pocket of gold. They were never able to find it again and neither has anybody else to this day.

Of course there is still the matter of the camel tracks on Banjo Burch's land. There is another camel legend which I am afraid to tell him because Banjo frightens rather easily.

There was this one time a bunch of prospectors found a fellow miner's corpse in the desert. They did not know his name but they held a funeral service and got drunk in his honor. Some time during the night one of the prospectors managed to capture a camel. The drunken miners took the dead prospector and lashed him to the camels back like a jockey. The skeleton supposedly stayed on the camel's back for years, the parts falling off one by one until just the legs and pelvis were left lashed to the camel. The skeleton camel jockey is often considered Arizona's grisly version of the *Legend of the Headless Horseman*. The bad news for my friend Banjo is the tracks on his land are more likely to belong to bewildered bovines or confused cattle than they are the last of Arizona's wild camels.

chapter 31:
Apache Horses

It was Coronado who brought the first horses into the land of the Gran Apacheria. We have no record of what the Apache thought at their first look at this new animal. As Coronado traveled through the mountains and valleys of what is now Arizona, his caravan traveled day after day, week after week, without seeing any local residents.

In their journals, the Spaniards dismissed this lush landscape as deserted and unpopulated. It was the heart of the Apache country and the people hid behind mountain boulders watching Coronado's cavalcade. The Apache peoples must have been awed by the size of Coronado's expedition made up of hundreds of conquistadors, settlers, and brides. Thousands of livestock including cattle, sheep, and horses, followed along, raising a cloud of dust behind the expedition which could be seen for miles.

When Coronado pulled his troops and wagons into a camp at the ancient abandoned ruins of Casa Malpais, Coronado's herders used the *kiva* there (the largest *kiva* in Arizona) as a pen for their sheep. The Native Americans who occupied near by Raven Village were so disgusted by this disrespect that they left their village and scattered to places that had never heard of Spaniards.

The New Mexico Native Americans were afraid of Coronado's horses. They were afraid the large beasts which the Spaniards loved to ride into battle were giant carnivores with a taste for human flesh. When the conquistadors had worn out their welcome in the pueblos, the expedition was tricked and sent to the great plains in a search for the bogus mythical kingdom of Quivira.

It was somewhere near Kansas that the exploring Spaniards finally ran into their first band of Apache, buffalo hunters known as the Lipan Apache. The Spaniards reported that the Apache people responded calmly to the horses, "approaching the horses and anointing themselves with their sweat." Historian Alexander Hartley writes of the incident that he was amazed that the Apache smeared their bodies with the fluid, doubtless with the idea of transferring to themselves something of the magic of the Great Dog of the white men.

The theme of the horse as a giant fierce dog appears again and again in first contact stories between the Spaniards and the Native Americans of the southwest. There is one story about a wandering conquistador who stopped for rest at a Pima village and asked the residents to please feed and water his steed. The next day the horse collapsed and died in the desert. When the conquistador returned he was furious but the Pima tried to explain. They had tried to feed the horse. They had offered it all sorts of meat; venison, javelina, rabbit, antelope, and quail, but the Great Dog of the Spanish had refused to eat.

No one is certain of the exact dates the Apache tribes acquired and domesticated horses. None of those Native Americans who saw Coronado bring the first horses to North America would ever ride one but their grandchildren saw an equine revolution which changed the Apache culture forever. Spanish journals say the Indians began mounted raids by the 1630s. These new beasts of burden made a nomadic people extremely mobile.

The U. S, Army officers who fought against them described the Apache soldiers as the best cavalry fighters in the world. Soldiers who had been all around the world would make comparisons to see how Apache mounted warriors stacked up against the Sioux, Russian Cossacks, and even themselves. Always, the Apache were declared the best horse riders in the world.

Apache horses grazing

It was the Apache cultural hero, Slayer of Enemies, who, legends say, made the first horse. Slayer of Enemies wanted a steed to ride into battle. First he tried to ride a deer, but no matter how hard he tried the deer would not listen. So Slayer of Enemies rode an antelope next and, while it was fast enough, the antelope was not strong enough to carry a full grown man. Next he rode an elk. The creature was plenty strong enough but was far too slow to be effective in battle. Javelina . . . let's just say there is nothing dignified about riding a *javelina* into battle. This is why Slayer of Enemies decided it was necessary to make an animal.

Slayer of Enemies took cornstalks and bent them into shape to form the skeleton. That is why the skeleton of the horse is jointed like a cornstalk. The soapy substance which forms from *agave* after a good rain was used to make horse sweat, the same horse sweat the Lipan blessed themselves with. Hailstones were used to make the teeth. Slayer of Enemies took lightning to give the horse a fiery breath. The hooves were made of rainbows and an arrowhead was attached to the bottom of each one so that the horse would have a powerful kick. Slayer of Enemies took a pair of crescent moons and formed the ears. For the eyes he chipped off a piece of the Morning Star. All that remained was to bring his creation to life. To accomplish this, Slayer of Enemies took four whirlwinds, one from each of the four directions and threw them inside.

The four directions play an important part in Apache mythology. The Sun keeps a corral with four horses; one for each of the cardinal points of the compass. Each direction has a color and a stone associated with it. For instance, the Black Horse has long been favored by Apache riders. It is usually called Black Wind Horse and is said to be linked to the stone jet. A black horse with a white face is said to be extremely intelligent and is the type Slayer of Enemies rides into battle. The red horse of the south is made of carnelian stone and the blue horse from the west is composed of turquoise. The favorite horse of the sun however is the horse of the east – the white horse. The white horse is made of seashell and every morning arises to lift the sun, in all her burning glory, up to her spot atop the heavens, bringing with it the break of a new day. According to Apache legend, the colors of the sunrise come from the fires of the sun being reflected in the white iridescence of the seashell horse.

Even today, the horse still holds a special place in Apache culture. In the summer, when I escape the desert summer heat by going trout fishing in the White Mountains, my automobile drives through reservation towns like Whiteriver, Hon Da, and McNary, I always turn my radio dial to the reservation radio and it seems like I always hear at least an hour or two of the rodeo news. Imagine that – an hour or two a day of the rodeo news. That is a lot of talk about horses.

chapter 32:
Apache Gaan Dancers

At a Tucson cultural festival the crowned dancers stretch and warm up. Each of the dancers is painted ashen white and decorated with black symbols depicting rain and lightning. Cloth masks cover their faces, while wooden crowns rise above their heads, sticks pointing up in all directions. Like their painted bodies, each crown is unique to each individual dancer. The Gaan dancers hold wooden sticks in each hand, which they click together rhythmically while they dance, swirling and twirling.

The appearance of the Gaan Dancers onstage causes the audience to buzz with excitement. There is a higher concentration of Native American faces in the crowd for this event. There are children of all colors sitting on the floor along the front row, waiting expectantly.

Big Jim Griffith, local folklorist and founder of the Tucson Meet Yourself Festival, introduces the leader of the Gaan dancers, a man who has brought dancers to perform at the festival every year since its inception. Dressed traditionally, the Apache leader Edgar Perry announces that this year is special because he just retired from teaching high school. He says he really enjoys being retired but drawls the vowels so that it sounds like he says "I enjoy being retarded." The audience chuckles along. He begins the performance by singing the *Star Spangled Banner* in the Apache language. A drummer joins the former history teacher on stage and together they begin the first song while the Gaan start to dance.

There is a story about how the Gaan first came to the Apache. A little boy was out deer hunting with his dog. They climbed high atop a mountain when they heard drumming and music. They followed the echoes of the pounding beat for miles. The boy and the dog discovered a small cave, way up high near the peak. The boy and the dog crept close and looking inside they could see the Gaan dancing around a bonfire.

The boy started to enter the cave. The dog barked and whined, refusing to go inside. The boy entered the cave anyways and the dog ran away with his tail between his legs. When the dog came home without the boy, his mother grew afraid. As the dog barked, the village followed, eager to rescue the boy. The dog led them to the mountain cave. The mother did not enter the cave but called to the Gaan to help her find her son.

The dog ran to one of the Gaan, leaping up and down. The dog had recognized his master. The boy's mother ran forward, tugging and tugging on her son's mask but it would not come off. The boy had become one of the Gaan.

While his mother cried, the boy tried to reassure her. Now that he was one of the Gaan, the mountain spirits would have a special relationship with the Apache people. Whenever Apache dancers donned the Gaan costumes and sang with a pure heart the Gaan would come to aid them.

The drummer at the festival keeps a steady beat, tapping his crook-shaped stick against the surface of his water-filled drum. The retired history teacher sings into the microphone; his voice proud and steady. The Gaan dancers click their two wooden sticks together in rhythm to the beat. There is the pounding of the shuffling feet and the jangle of the bells on the belts and moccasins. Gaan dancing is hard work and soon the sweaty dancers add their labored breathing to the music, snorting and gasping like horses in a rodeo. The Gaan swirl and twirl, in a flurry of motion.

When they must rest, the Gaan place the points of their sticks upon the ground. They arch their backs and tilt back their heads with crowns pointing backwards. The silhouettes remind me of bugling elk but the sounds which erupt from their masked faces are unearthly. The Gaan dancers whistle, shriek, howl, yowl, trill, and growl as they summon the mountain spirits. The children in the front row watch, mesmerized and slightly frightened.

There are three grown men dressed as Gaan dancers; one trim athlete, one with a substantial Buddha belly, and one in between. There is also a little Apache boy, learning the trade as a clown. The presence of the audience seems to intimidate and frighten the little boy. Not quite so shy is one of the

Gaan Dancers show their stances and their costumes.

granddaughters of the history teacher who approaches him on the stage. He never misses a beat, continuing to sing as he bends down to pick up his grand daughter (or great granddaughter), holding her while he finishes the song. He explains the next song and when the drummer pounds the first beat the Gaan dancers erupt into another flurry of rhythm and motion, the bells rattling on their legs. The little girl waves softly to the crowd while her grandfather sings. The Gaan dancers prance and sway. The show ends with the history teacher singing *God Bless America* in the Apache language and asking for a prayer to protect our soldiers overseas.

The next performers take the stage quickly, hoping to take advantage of the large audience. A troupe of percussionists play a Japanese-style of drumming known as *taiko*. The drummers flail with flamboyant powerful swings of the arms. Next is a Japanese horse song. As the drums imitate the rhythms of a galloping stallion, I notice some Apache children giggling. The Apache understand horses and the brown-skinned children begin to clap. Soon the entire audience joins in. It is almost as if the Gaan are smiling as they gallop away, riding rhythmic mustangs.

chapter 33:
Waila Music

Angelo Joaquin Jr. says he has memories of being driven all over the far flung O'odham reservation on holidays. Sometimes his father's popular dance band would play four dances in four nights, crisscrossing the unpaved roads of a reservation the same size as Connecticut. Elder Waila players have been known to tell younger musicians that they have the responsibility to use their talents to make people happy. Angelo's father was a musical pioneer, founding one of the original Waila bands.

At a November 2004 lecture at the Arizona Historical Society, Angelo Joaquin Jr. recalled those long drives to Waila festivals. The whole family would be crowded into the car. Stretching across all the seats, both front and back, was uncle Leonard's bass fiddle. The kids in the family grew up with bent necks from dodging the giant bass as it bounced along the bumpy reservation roads. Uncle Leonard was a teenager at the time and needed to stand on a box to reach the neck of the giant instrument. Leonard was happier than anybody when electricity came to the reservation and he could finally play a lightweight electric bass.

A traditional Waila band is usually composed of two alto saxophones, a button accordion, electric guitar, electric bass, and drum kit. Waila music is almost entirely instrumental and consists mostly of polkas, two steps, and *cumbias*. This is definitely dance music. Many Waila musicians describe their style as *norteno* music with an O'odham accent.

Sometimes you will hear Waila music described as *Chicken Scratch*. This is because many people dance to *waila* with hands behind their back and kicking up their heels like chickens scratching. Everybody dances in a long, slow, counterclockwise circle. The songs tend to be long; they need to last all night.

O'odham band performing chicken scratch music

Dancing is the heart and soul of Waila music. Some performers compare waila festivals to the Native American round dances; a social event designed to promote tribal unity. O'odham feet shuffle across the desert earth, slowly twirling in a counter clockwise circle. There is no right or wrong way to dance to Waila music, some people chicken scratch, some couples twirl together while other couples hold each other close and move slowly. Long strings of children will hold hands and skip around the circle or even chase each other. Angelo says that one of his favorite parts of Waila festivals is when everybody has been dancing together for hours to the same rhythms, twirling in the same circle for hours, and you just know that everybody's heart is beating as one.

The tradition of popular music among the O'odham predates Waila by almost a century. Before Waila there were O'odham fiddle bands. The violins were introduced to the O'odham by missionaries for use in church and to usurp traditional native music. A typical O'odham fiddle band would consist of two violins, a guitar, snare drum, and bass drum. The earliest reference to an O'odham fiddle band comes from the 1860s when a newspaper account mentions a fiddle band performing at the Tucson presidio. As the oldest generation of O'odham fiddlers is passing away there is a very real fear that the songs will die out without being passed on.

The Joaquin Brothers Waila Band was formed in 1947 in Los Angeles, California, of all places. As part of the Assimilation Act, Native Americans were encouraged to move to large metropolitan areas such as Phoenix, Los Angeles, and Chicago. Angelo senior moved to Los Angeles and, after he got established, he sent for the rest of the family. Angelo junior grew up in a household where English was a second language. In fact his grandmother and great grandmother lived in the same house and did not speak English at all. Los Angeles came as quite a shock to the whole family. In order to keep tribal bonds and traditions together, Angelo senior would get together with two cousins who had enlisted in the military service as Marines at nearby Camp Pendleton. They would play music in the afternoon. When the family moved back to the Tohono, (the traditional desert lands of the O'odham) Uncle Leonard was added to the band and the Waila revolution was underway.

The way Angelo Jr. describes those early days, they have a romantic feel. Waila dances are held at night, avoiding the hundred degree plus temperatures of an Arizona summer day. Typically these fiestas lasted from sundown to sunrise. Waila music is played in high keys because it carries further across the desert landscape at night. The O'odham say that the thin, scraggly, bark of the creosote bushes amplifies the music over the desert. The dances would start by an elder sprinkling water on the earthen dance floors to keep the dust down. Lights and amplifiers were run by generators but cars would circle the dance floor so that if the generator ran out of gas, the fiesta could continue. The parked cars would take turns lighting the dance floor before their batteries drained.

Most of those early gigs for the Joaquin Brothers were in one of two places; bars or churches. Dancers and musicians were equally at home in both venues. The same songs are played for fiestas and funerals; they are just a little slower and in a minor key for a funeral. Much has changed over the decades, waila bands have played all over the country including New York and Wolf Trap. Angelo junior described watching his father's band play at a folk festival in Los Angeles. The stage was up against the ocean and he talked about the irony of this desert music being played next to all that water.

There is a waila festival held every year at Bear Down Field at the University of Arizona. Angelo Joaquin junior is one of the original founders of this festival hosted by the Arizona Historical Society. The idea was to do more than keep the musical traditions of the O'odham alive but also to expose this festive music to a larger audience.

Traditional foods such as cholla buds, saguaro syrup, and tepary beans are served; not just to expose these foods to an urban audience but to remind young O'odham of them when their families no longer harvest the desert. At every Waila Festival since the inception of the event in 1989, O'odham elders have been bused into Tucson from the reservation to lend their presence to the proceedings. The festivals are always fun, big groups of people dancing together and spinning in a long, slow, counterclockwise circle.

The spontaneous unity and camaraderie the dancers experience is one of the main reasons the festival is held. There are still many older O'odham who remember being taught as young children in the 20s and 30s to run and hide in the desert at the sound of an approaching automobile. Cars were rare on the reservation back then and no Indian owned one. Any approaching automobile must belong to a government agent or missionary who was likely to kidnap the children and take them away to boarding school. The waila festival is held to overcome these types of historic suspicion and mistrust. Angelo Joaquin remembers asking one of the elders what she thought of all the *merigans* (the O'odham word for American) dancing to waila music.

She smiled and said, "They are not so bad after all."

The author at age ten playing his saxophone

chapter 34:
Old Instruments & Forgotten Melodies

The retired German professor dies and his daughter gives me a gift of old instruments. Her father loved to visit antique shops and acquire ancient musical instruments. I receive a transverse flute, mechanically intricate and shiny, even if it is slightly used. There is an old wooden clarinet that makes me want to summon the ghost of Benny Goodman, but all I can do is make it honk like a goose. Best of all is a flute and piccolo set, long slender black lacquered wood bodies topped with bone mouthpieces. Who knows how old they are? I was a marching-band nerd all through high school and I never saw any instruments with wood bodies and bone mouthpieces.

These new old instruments will go well with the one I already own. I am lucky enough to possess a beautiful silver saxophone, gift of my grandfather, a treasure scavenged from an attic. My saxophone was purchased used during the roaring 20s, produced by a midwestern factory which would go belly up during the Great Depression. My saxophone was played by my grandfather in speakeasy dance halls.

My beautiful silver saxophone served as a rhythmic prohibition prophet to flappers and dapper dudes in a basement gin joint run by my great uncle. My great-uncle Frank was a lifelong railroad man who used his management position to run rum all across the United States. My grandfather did not care about the illegal activities, he just knew that he was getting paid to play music, participating in the birth of jazz. In the audience, gangsters, molls, dolls, and birds danced and flapped frenetically. Sometimes Al Capone would be in attendance. He would listen and applaud while chomping on fine cigars and sipping good whiskey.

My grandfather is not a blood relative, none of my

relations are. I was put up for adoption at eight-months old. I have only a few vague memories of my birth mother. I seem to recall some faint warm memories of being held but I have no idea if these feelings are real or tender imaginary fantasies. A few years ago I exercised some of my legal rights and acquired what is known as a non-identifying letter. So I know a few obscure things. It's like putting together a jigsaw puzzle without any idea of the whole picture. For instance, I know that I was born at The University of Arizona on a sorority house floor.

My mother had tried to hide her pregnancy (such things were very scandalous back then) by wearing a tight girdle. It was right there in my medical records because my pediatrician thought the girdle might explain my terrible temper as an infant. After being born at the sorority house, I was whisked off to St. Joseph's Hospital and given a name. It is not the name I wear now. At eight months old I was put up for adoption after a bitter legal batter. My birth mother had wanted to put me up for adoption almost immediately. It was my grandmother who wanted to keep custody of me, so she sued . . . and lost. That was when Noel Eric Streitmatter ceased to be.

I became a poster child. My friends will tell you that it is obvious that my picture should be on a poster somewhere pleading with the general public to prevent people like me. My editor might even tell you the same thing. It is true though, as a tiny baby I was a poster child for the Arizona Children's Home. I am wrapped in a blanket, all smiles. My real mom's hand and arm are visible as she reaches out to touch me. The day that picture was taken is the day I became Gary Every.

I am lucky to have the family I have. I am close to all my brothers and sisters. My nephews and nieces are all wonderful amazing human beings. Still, I can't help but wonder what sort of genetic surprises await me as I get older. What personality traits are uniquely me and which are handed down through the family, generation after generation? Mostly, I wonder if those warm memories of being held are real or imagined.

I do know one more piece of obscure trivia about my birth family. My great grandmother was a clarinetist in the original Tucson Symphony Orchestra. One day, celebrating some sort of symphony anniversary, there was a photograph in the newspaper of the original orchestra. I clipped the picture out of the paper and saved it. I am certain that the picture still exists somewhere in my house, even if I could not tell you which drawer or closet box it is hiding inside. Sometimes memories are like that. You become certain of them even if you are not sure exactly what they are or where they came from. I do remember rather vividly, staring at the symphony photograph and trying to figure out which musician I was descended from. In my mind, I can still see the faces of the pretty young women in the photograph, wearing beautiful gowns and proudly holding thin black lacquered clarinets in their hands. These are things I think about while cleaning beautiful antique instruments, the gift of a dead man I barely knew. I am trying to listen to the echoes of some long forgotten melodies.

Ripe saguaro fruit

chapter 35:
O'odham New Year

For more than 8,000 years the Tohono O'odham have been celebrating their own unique version of the New Year in the Sonoran Desert. For 8,000 years the drums have beat, the voices have risen in song, and the people have danced until sunrise as they celebrated.

Our culture notes the New Year on January 1st but the Tohono O'odham use the opposite end of the calendar. The traditional Tohono O'odham New Year takes place in July. If you visit the reservation during the first week in July you might get a glimpse of preparations and festivities taking place in villages such as Sells, Topawa, Santa Rosa or Gu Achi.

The O'odham New Year is centered on the saguaro fruit harvest. The saguaro cactus is the jolly green giant of the Sonoran Desert, towering 50 or 60 feet into the air. The old-time cowboys used to say that the ancient Indians believed that each and every saguaro held the spirit of a dead warrior and that every arm represented a wife. Saguaro arms pointed up to the heavens represented happy and faithful wives but the occasional down turned arm meant a domestic problem. Like many aphorisms that begin, "The old-time cowboys used to say that the ancient Indians believed . . ." there are some problems. My friend Erica pointed out that she was bothered that a chief with many lovers could have one of those women be accused of infidelity.

A down-turned saguaro arm is an indication of frost damage at the elbow. The weight of the cactus will point the arm downward. If the cactus lives long enough, the arm will eventually turn upwards once more. If you want, you can use that as a metaphor for the power of love to heal.

One O'odham legend about the creation of the saguaro begins during a terrible drought when the people were faced with famine and certain death. A mother went to sleep and had a dream. When she awoke she told her children that she knew how to rescue the desert people. The mother demanded that her children bury her in the sand. When the first monsoon raindrops struck the soil she emerged as a full grown saguaro complete with blossoms and fruit to feed her starving children, and with arms to hug them.

When April arrives the saguaros begin to bloom; bouquets of flowers appear at the end of every arm and at the top of every crown. The saguaro blossom is the state flower. The four-inch long white flowers have a bright yellow center which smells faintly of cantaloupe. Saguaro flowers are pollinated by insects and birds but the dominant pollinator of the saguaro flower is the Mexican long nosed bat. If you view the winged mammals as they feed at the saguaro flowers you will notice their little bat faces are sticky with yellow pollen.

By mid May the flower petals have begun falling and the green node the flowers are perched atop gradually turn into ripening fruit. As it ripens, the outside of the saguaro fruit slowly darkens until it resembles a crisp blackened banana peel. You know the fruit is ripe when it splits open and reveals the red pulp jelly inside. Many first time visitors to the desert mistake the ripe fruit for the flowers because the saguaro cactus looks like it is covered by ugly roses when the fruit splits open to reveal the red jelly inside.

The saguaro fruit ripen around the first week in July, just when the monsoon season reaches the Sonoran Desert. A drive through the O'odham reservation this time of year often reveals families roaming the desert hillsides. Usually there are one or two O'odham grandmothers in charge of the operation, sometimes in traditional dress such as cotton blouses and skirts. There are also a host of Native American daughters, nephews, nieces, sons, and a variety of grandchildren, wandering the desert hillsides gathering saguaro fruit.

To harvest saguaro fruit one uses a wooden rib from the skeleton of a dead saguaro. A small cross stick is placed at the end of the long pole. One of the grandmothers approaches a giant cactus and knocks the clusters of fruit free. Except it takes more energy than that, a running start is required, followed by a lunging thrust and a grunt (it helps to grunt). Then saguaro fruit is launched every which way through the air. It is like breaking open a cactus *pinata*.

There is a reason why saguaro fruit harvesting is a matriarchal tradition. If you are a grandmother, that means there are plenty of grandchildren to pick up the scattered saguaro fruit, wherever it lands. It would become tiring to drop your 50-foot-long pole, stoop over to gather the saguaro fruit, and then bend over to pick up your pole again, in order to knock more fruit from the cacti and repeat the process again. Instead the grandchildren gather the fruit as the old women continue to whack cactus. The O'odham children are doing more than keeping grandmother's back from getting sore and tired, they are keeping alive an ancient tradition.

The best parts of everyone's saguaro fruit harvest are donated to a community pool. Everybody's contribution is placed into a large pot and boiled down into saguaro fruit wine. The cactus fruit wine is sugary sweet and a bright red color, just perfect for the ceremonial symbolism. For thousands of years, saguaro fruit wine was the only alcoholic beverage the O'odham made and for thousands of years the only time the people were allowed to drink it was during the New Years ceremony. It was quite a bacchanalia festival. The O'odham people would drum, dance, and sing all night long.

At sunrise would come the sacred part of the ceremony. That was when the desert people would fan out across the landscape and attempt to capture frogs. The ripening of saguaro fruit also coincides with the shift of our weather patterns to the beginning of the monsoons. Technically speaking, our desert amphibians do not practice the art of hibernation. Hibernation is when animals sleep to escape the cold of winter, but our desert amphibians go dormant to avoid the scorching hot, dry summers. Sleeping in the summer is known as *estivation*. There are as many as 30 species of frogs and toads who burrow underground to escape the dry summer heat, only to emerge following the first monsoon storm of the summer. As residents of the Sonoran Desert will attest, these newly awakened amphibians sing with a loud and lusty enthusiasm. They are in a hurry to meet and court Mrs. Frog while there are still rain puddles and water holes left for the eggs and tadpoles to grow in. While the frogs are hopping and singing, the desert people try to capture them.

Catching a frog while even slightly intoxicated is a difficult thing to do, but after a night of drinking sweet red saguaro wine it becomes nearly impossible. The celebrating O'odham chase the renegade amphibians with lots of mirthful giggling. Once the frogs are captured they are never harmed but cradled carefully with both hands and held up to the heavens. Then the celebrants pray for rain.

Even as the desert people enjoy the saguaro fruit harvest (their cactus mother once again saving them from famine) they are aware that if the monsoons do not come soon and rain hard there will be no corn or beans to harvest in the autumn. The drums beat, the dancers shuffle, and the voices rise in song. The words are carried upwards by the arms of the giant saguaro, green arms reaching all the way into the sky, carrying the lyrical words into the heavens. Their dreams swimming in a sea of red wine, the O'odham people ask the frogs to bless us with good monsoons.

Happy New Year!

chapter 36:
The Quijotoa Ghost

The town of Oracle began as a series of scattered mining camps on the north slopes of the Santa Catalina mountain range. The miners formed a loose knit community without a name until 1878 when a Scotsman named Alexander McKay arrived. McKay came to work the mining claim of his good friend Albert Weldon. Weldon had named his mining claim after his uncle's ship, the H.M.S. Oracle, which had brought Weldon to America. The next year McKay built what he claimed was, "The first house in Oracle, a one room adobe for me and Weldon."

Although the mine on the north slope of the mountains yielded a profit and gave a name to the frontier town, the two friends continued prospecting. They were always searching for the one great strike which would make them wealthy beyond their wildest dreams. There was a method to McKay's madness. The wandering Scot would prospect the desert lowlands in the winter, avoiding the worst of the blistering heat. In the summer he would prospect the mountain highlands, avoiding the cold and snow.

In the winter of 1879, McKay prospected along the Mexican border. McKay claim-staked a small cap of rock which showed signs of iron. Three years later, Weldon was examining the claim and discovered some copper ore with traces of silver just beneath the surface. The men decided to investigate the region further. To get a better view of the area, McKay and his companions climbed Quijotoa Peak. The view from the top of the peak revealed little.

A sudden gust of wind blew Alexander McKay's hat from his head and over the precipice. Fearful, that the Arizona summer sun would burn his fair-skinned, bald, head, McKay asked his companions to assist him with retrieving his hat.

The men used a long rope to lower McKay down the length of the cliff. After capturing the wayward hat, McKay asked the men to pause him in the middle of the cliff. McKay used his pocket knife to scrape the rocks. When he had been returned to the top of the mountain McKay showed the tiny pieces of silver ore he had discovered and proudly exclaimed; "Gentleman, the Comstock of Arizona is atop this mountain."

Quijotoa is an O'odham word meaning mountain shaped like basket. Today the mountain slopes are surrounded by miles of uninhabited desert. For many millennia the countryside has remained quiet and solitary but, for a brief period, the slopes of Quijotoa were home to a bustling boomtown. The silver ore McKay had discovered assayed out at $3,600 dollars to the ton. McKay and Weldon staked The Peerless Mine and the Quijotoa silver rush had begun.

A new town called Logan City suddenly appeared on the sides of the steep mountain slopes. The sharply tilted new town was described by one writer as having "the finest drainage of any town on the Pacific Coast." San Francisco capitalist, W. S. Lyle just happened to drop by the remote desert mines and soon contacted other investors with good news. Men who had grown wealthy on the silver mined from Nevada's Comstock Lode, men such as James C. Flood and John Mackey, quickly invested in the Quijotoa mines. The investors soon raised $50,000,000 dollars in capital stock.

The population skyrocketed. The new towns of Virginia City, New Virginia, and Brooklyn were laid out contiguous to Logan City. On the opposite side of the mountain, General J. B. "Pie" Allen founded Allen City. Industry soon followed with stagecoach lines, hardware stores, lodging houses, and a variety of saloons. The *Phoenix Gazette* reported on January 6, 1884, "Drinking water is quoted from 50 to 70 cents a bucket. It is surprising that saloons can afford to furnish liquor at 12 and one-half cents with water commanding such a high figure . . ."

The Arizona Silver Belt, a newspaper based out of Globe, wrote about the new mining boom town, "They are putting up some good buildings of lumber and canvas. No adobes are made as water is too scarce. It has to be hauled from five to ten miles away and sells at ten cents a gallon." It was unusual for an Arizona frontier town to be built of timber. The lack of adobe and water would come back to haunt the new community later.

During one six month period in 1884 more than 1,500 mining locations were claim staked. Men began to compare the Quijotoa mining strike with the discovery of gold at Sutter's Mill in California. The jubilation didn't last very long however. When the rich scabbing of ore located on the mountain top had been harvested the mine began to dry up. Seeking a new ore body, the mining company drilled a tunnel all the way through the mountain. The only thing the tunnel revealed was daylight at the other end. Millions and millions of dollars had been poured into the mountain and about half a million had been pulled back out.

The future of Quijotoa lay in the hands of a few hopeful prospectors who scoured the desert searching for the next big strike that would revitalize the community. Disaster struck on June 19, 1889 when a fire began. Without any water to fight the blaze, the town built entirely of wood and canvas was consumed by flames in little more than an hour.

Without the mines open there seemed little sense in rebuilding the towns along the slopes of Quijotoa. Logan City, Virginia City, New Virginia, and Brooklyn were all reduced to ghost towns. The ghost appeared quickly enough.

On the morning of the fire, three road-weary and sullen men arrived only to discover that the boomtown had just gone bust. The three men were seated at a table in Mrs. Stewart's restaurant when the fire broke out. After the fire extinguished itself the survivors gathered and the three strangers were nowhere to be seen. It was feared the newcomers had perished in the blaze.

As the years passed, prospectors would roam the region, hoping to discover pockets of overlooked riches. Men reported hearing weird noises and bells ringing in the midst of the abandoned ruins. One party of four men pulled up camp in the middle of the night after listening for hours to the moans and groans of a dying man. In 1896 a man named Ed Whipple dragged himself to the local sheriff to report that he had been captured and held prisoner by an eccentric hermit. The bearded hermit lived in one of the abandoned mine shafts and kept a human skeleton on the mantle piece. The hermit held long conversations with the skull, that he referred to as Silver.

The hermit was taken to jail where he attacked the prison trusty in charge of bringing food to the different cells. The hermit was interrogated about his motivation for his violent attack upon his fellow inmate. Questioning revealed the hermit was named Fred McComb and the trusty was John Cronkhite. The two men had known each other back in Nebraska, where, with a third man named Matt Silver, they had robbed and murdered a farmer before heading out for the Quijotoa silver boom. The outlaws had arrived in Quijotoa just in time to discover that the mines had closed only days before and the men arrived only minutes before the fire began.

In the confusion of the conflagration, Cronkhite shot Silver before running off with the stolen money. Cronkhite escaped amidst the leaping flames. McComb took his injured friend and slipped away unseen into a mine shaft. Matt Silver never recovered from his gunshot wounds. After his companion's untimely demise, McComb wrapped the corpse in chicken wire "so the rats couldn't get him." It was after this that McComb started his ghostly moans, midnight bell ringing, and murderous screams to hide his mountain refuge.

Reunited unexpectedly with Cronkhite in prison, McComb tried to avenge the death of Matt Silver. A query sent to the Nebraska legal system revealed that there were no longer any witnesses alive left to testify against the two men in the murder of the farmer, so extradition was not requested. McComb and Cronkhite were released from prison and it is said that McComb returned to haunt the ghost towns along Quijotoa for perhaps as long as 15 more years. There was no word on what happened to the skull of his conversational companion Mr. Silver.

Raven Butte, Cabeza Prieta Wilderness

chapter 37:
The Ghost of Melchior Diaz

The Sierra Pinacate volcanic range is quickly gaining a reputation as one of the most exotic landscapes on the planet. It is located only a short distance from the ocean shores of *Puerto Penasco* (Rocky Point). This ancient volcanic field holds one of the earth's driest deserts. The area averages only two to four inches of rain a year and one giant crater went seven years without recorded rain.

As one might expect, the plants of the Pinacates reflect the tough conditions. One of the most southern reaches of the Sonoran Desert, the landscape is still dotted with saguaros. Much more common are the thick fields of teddy-bear *cholla* which populate the cinder cone slopes like an army of tiny, thorny soldiers. There are only a few scattered organ pipe cacti, but there are many of the fuzzy crested senita. Particularly exotic are the multi-headed barrel cactus with interlocking thorns that protect the plants from grazing herbivores.

The geology itself looks fire blasted; the rocks appear to be just out of the furnace as lava flows sprawl in twisted shapes. Cinder cones holding gigantic craters erupt all across the landscape. The largest of these is Crater Elegante, over 800 feet deep and 4,800 feet in diameter. Some of the lava flows are colored rust red but most of them are jet black. All of them are striking when the glistening white sand dunes spill across them. Early Spanish pioneers named this path the *Camino Diablo* or Devil's Road.

The first Old World explorer to travel the Camino Diablo was Melchior Diaz in 1540. Diaz was a part of the Coronado expedition as it tried to find lost cities of gold.

Coronado had thought it was possible that his colony in New Mexico could be supplied by sea. Hernando Alarcon was given a ship and the best approximate directions possible to try and locate Coronado. California turned out not to be an island, and Alarcon was forced to try and navigate the Colorado River upstream. Men walked along both sides of the shore, connected to the sailing vessel by ropes as they towed the heavy vessel northward. Alarcon gave up near the junction of the Gila and Colorado River without reaching Coronado and without imagining the Grand Canyon which still lay as an obstacle up ahead. Coronado sent Melchior Diaz along the Camino Diablo to try and locate Alarcon.

The irony that Diaz became the first explorer to cross this dry and brutal desert in an attempt to reach the ocean has never ceased to amaze me. Melchior Diaz traveled this region of cactus thorns, cinder cones, and sand dunes accompanied by a half dozen conquistadors and a flock of 40 sheep. You can imagine how delighted the wolves were by this banquet of mutton on the hoof. The gray wolves must have practically drooled as they watched the plump domesticated sheep march through this inhospitable desert. The wolves howled all night while the lost conquistadors huddled by the fire and the sheep circled around, bleating nervously.

In the morning Melchior Diaz prepared for battle. The proud conquistador donned his armor and mounted his stallion. With lance in hand, he charged into the fray, jousting the feral canine carnivores. Atop his galloping steed, Diaz eyed the kill and lunged . . .

The wolf dodged and the blade of the lance struck nothing but stone. The butt of the spear bounced back and fatally wounded the exploring conquistador. Melchior Diaz lay in the shade, slowly dying from a self-inflicted groin wound, painfully aware that he was suffering perhaps the most inglorious death in all of history.

No one has ever found the lost grave of Melchior Diaz. It is one of the great mysteries of the region. The grave is so lost that no one can even say for certain whether Melchior Diaz' remains are in the Sierra Pinacate, Gran Desierto, Cabeza Prieta Wilderness, or Organ Pipe National Monument. What is worth noting is, that when combined, these four bioreserves, (Two on the American side and two on the Mexican side) make up the second-largest wilderness preserve on the planet. Perhaps it will soon be the largest, depending on the extent of drilling in the Arctic Wilderness Refuge.

Sad to say, the last Mexican gray wolf disappeared from the Pinacates in the 1970s. According to unconfirmed reports, a funny thing has happened since the wolves went extinct from the region. On full-moon nights you can sometimes hear the ghosts of the wolves howl. Sometimes you can even see their shadows, just their shadows, racing across the landscape, feral ghost dogs running wild.

Suddenly the sand will shift, the earth will open, and the grave of Melchior Diaz opens wide. The ghost of Melchior Diaz rises up from the earth still riding atop his magnificent stallion, lance in his hand, preparing to battle wolves once more. The horse gallops into the darkness as the ghost wolves flee before it and Melchior Diaz aims his lance, shouting out the conquistador battle cry of "Santiago! Santiago!"

Female adventurers are safe from this ghost when they travel the Camino Diablo but male travelers must be especially wary, because like Ichabod Crane's headless horseman, the ghost of Melchior Diaz seeks to replace that which he has lost and we all know just which particular body parts the ghost of Melchior Diaz no longer carries.

chapter 38:
Terrenate

Terrenate is the site of a failed Spanish presidio and can be reached with a short hike (2.4 miles round trip) through the San Pedro Riparian Zone. The trail follows an old railroad grade and makes for easy walking. The BLM has put in plenty of benches for the weary to sit and rest. Those hikers who take advantage of the benches will want to enjoy the views of the Dragoon, Whetstone, Huachuca, Chiricuahua Mountains on the horizon. The trail crosses a flat field of desert-scrub bushes until it comes to the cliffs overlooking the San Pedro River. It is here that the ruins of the fortress Terrenate are located.

As you stand at the crumbled adobe walls of what used to be the main gate, imagine yourself entering the Presidio Santa Cruz de Terrenate in the year 1776. Listen for the intermingling of Spanish and Native American voices, listen to the history. Many of the structures have accompanying interpretive plaques explaining what the ruins used to be. Listen closely and you will hear the current of the river as it carves its course below the high cliffs, meandering from bank to bank in a wide sandy channel. Groves of huge cottonwood trees grow along the shores. The flowing river is one of the pleasures of the hike; no crowds – only the reassuring sounds of running water. If you look carefully you can see the footprints of deer, javelina, and raccoon in the soft sand.

One of the preserved ruins in the area are the adobe walls of the chapel or *"la capilla."* Established in 1776, the Presidio Santa Cruz de Terrenate's Church of the Holy Terrestrial Cross was abandoned by 1781. The priests at la capilla must have overseen much more tragedy than joy. Disease was rampant among the Native Americans of the community and the priests must have conducted the funerals for the soldiers who battled in the Apache wars. The Spanish and the Apache fought fiercely for control of the San Pedro River Valley.

The rectangular ruin ridges along the hilltops remind me of the Dragoon Mountains on the horizon. The remnants of the walls of the commander's quarters still stand nearly shoulder high. Atop the bastion you can still see the fortress tower where the Spanish soldiers fired cannons at approaching enemies. The presidio itself was never completed. The Apaches realized that if they allowed the protective outer wall to be finished, the Spanish would be able to control this vital corridor between so many mountains. The Apache warriors kept the Spanish workers under continual attack. The Spaniards employed two oxen for the task of hauling stones and other building supplies from the bottom of the river up the steep cliffs where the presidio was located. The Apache came up with a simple solution to stop the oxen – they ate them. It was a devastating blow to the construction project.

On July 7, 1776, after a fierce battle, Captain Francisco Tovar and 26 soldiers met a violent death. Ironically, on the other side of the continent, the Declaration of Independence had been signed only a few days earlier on July 4th. Over the next few years, 54 more Spanish soldiers and another captain would die at Terrenate. The Spanish conquistadors would never complete the presidio walls, never successfully harvest a crop, and by 1781 the frontier outpost was abandoned. There is a strange and lonely beauty which hovers over the ruins at Terrenate. If one listens to the wind you can almost hear the bells at the chapel of the Holy Terrestrial Cross ringing mournfully.

chapter 39:
The Lady in Blue

Father Kino, the exploring padre who roamed the southwest, encountered a mystery during his travels. Many of the remote places he explored, locations where he was frequently the first European to ever visit; the resident Native Americans had already been introduced to Christianity by a mysterious figure known only as *The Lady in Blue*. Father Kino recorded in his extensive journals that when he and his companions had traveled to the junction of the Gila and Colorado Rivers in 1699, they were told by the Native Americans who farmed and lived there, that a woman dressed in blue and carrying a cross had preached to their grandparents in a strange language.

The legends of the Lady in Blue spread throughout the southwest, reaching from what is now northern Mexico and southern Arizona all the way to east Texas and western Louisiana. In 1689, explorer Alonso de Leon and the Franciscan monk Damian Mazanet traveled the rolling woodland hills between the Trinity and Red Rivers. Leon described the Caddos peoples as living "in towns with wooden houses . . . and plant corn, beans, squash, watermelons, and melons." The reputation of the prosperous Caddoans reached as far as the Spanish missions of New Mexico who referred to it as the Kingdom of Tejas. Leon reported that the Caddos were yearning for Christianity; having been visited by the Lady in Blue some years before.

The story of the Lady in Blue began to grow among the missions of the Rio Grande Valley in New Mexico. It was said that she struck down a Taos sorceress with a thunderbolt. Plains Indians known to the Spaniards as the Apaches and Jumanos had told the Franciscans that a woman dressed like a nun had preached to them in their own languages. The

New Mexican friars did not know what to make of such a story.

Back in Spain, the mystery was about to get much more mystical. There were reports that a Franciscan nun named Sister Maria de Agreda from the order of Poor Clares of St. Francis had made spiritual journeys to North America. Sister Maria de Agreda was an anorexic young woman who used to fast until she had religious visions. Fray Alonzo de Benavides interviewed the beautiful 29-year-old abbess in 1631 and she described how, for the last decade, she had made visits to New Mexico. At the urging of Fray Alonzo she wrote a letter to the pueblo missions, recounting her numerous trips to New Mexico, "transported by the aid of angels" not only across the ocean but back in time as well. Fray Alonzo enthusiastically mailed a copy of the letter to the New Mexican friars; including his own interpretation of his conversation with the beautiful nun dressed in the Franciscan cloak and blue robes of her order.

By 1650, Sister Maria de Agreda was a woman of considerable political influence in Spain and she repudiated much of what she had told Fray Benavides, claiming that she had been misunderstood and badgered by her questioners. She even went so far as to burn her copy of her 1631 letter to the New Mexico missionaries. A lynch mob gathered. Sister Maria de Agreda left a glimmer of doubt for the faithful when she wrote, "I have always doubted that it was my actual body that went, but since there were so many eyewitness accounts," she concluded that, "It might have been an angel impersonating me."

The lynch mob dispersed. Sister Maria de Agreda's partial repudiation of the story was quickly forgotten and did not receive anywhere near the attention her original declaration had. In fact, over the ensuing centuries the legend of the Lady in Blue grew and grew until it attained mythic

'Lady in Blue' at the Sasco cemetery

proportions. The figure of the Lady in Blue was frequently spied helping the poor and oppressed and many time her actions were courageous and heroic.

Perhaps the most striking example of this is her role in the battle of Caborca. In 1850, an American rogue named Henry Crabb led an army of mercenaries out of Tucson, Arizona, and into northern Mexico, hoping to capture the border state of Sonora and establish his own miniature empire. The deciding battle took place in the town of Caborca with the invading mercenary army on one side of the plaza and the local residents holed up behind the thick adobe walls of the Caborcan mission. Again and again members of Crabb's army would brave gunfire to rush the mission doors, lighting and relighting the fuse atop the kegs of dynamite, only to have a courageous woman in a blue cloak come out from the church and snuff out the fuse again and again. No matter how many shots Crabb's best snipers took at the valiant woman she remained unscathed. No matter how many times the invaders attempted to blow up the church doors the Lady in Blue would extinguish the dynamite before it could explode.

The citizens of Caborca fought off Crabb's invading army until the cavalry came to rescue the day. The Mexican cavalry executed all of the surrendered soldiers except Charlie

Evans; the youngest member of Crabb's party at the tender age of 16. After the battle Evans confided to one of the local citizens that Crabb's army would have won the battle if they could have gotten inside the church. Then they could have held off the Mexican army. The courageous Lady in Blue had saved the day for the town of Caborca. A surprised Evans was later told that no Lady in Blue lived in the village.

The next significant reappearance of the Lady in Blue occurred deep in the heart of Mexico in the 1800s. A young Mayo woman named Teresa Urrea fell sick and "died" for 24 hours. When she awoke she acquired great fame as a healer. Many Mayo began to revere her as a saint. In 1892, while Teresa Urrea was curing at a *pasko* (fiesta), the Mexican army, fearing a rebellious uprising, attacked, shooting many of her followers. Miss Urrea and her family fled north across the border to Arizona.

Teresa Urrea and her family settled in Clifton, Arizona, where her reputation as a healer and miracle worker quickly grew. Some referred to her as *"Our Lady of the Gila"* and others thought her to be a reincarnation of the Lady in Blue. The beautiful 22-year-old woman placed her soft hands on the afflicted, closed her brown eyes, and intoned a prayer of healing. Although Saint Teresa always refused payment for her services, her father was known to linger in the living rooms after his daughter had left, gradually increasing the family wealth.

During the course of her visits, Teresa became acquainted with the handsome young Jose Rodriguez and soon romance blossomed. A date was set for a wedding in late August. Those who believed in Teresa Urrea's sainthood were shocked and appalled. They were stunned that anybody could think of committing the sacrilegious blasphemy of marrying a saint. On the wedding day an unruly mob gathered outside the church and threatened to riot. The

Clifton police arrived and arrested the groom on charges of insanity. They said, "He must be crazy to want to go through with this while a lynch mob is waiting outside the church." Teresa Urrea and her family fled to the City of Angels, Los Angeles, California, where she was never heard from again.

Although Teresa Urrea disappeared, the Lady in Blue has far from vanished. Folklorist "Big" Jim Griffith tells the tale of an O'odham woman who had a son enlisted in the U.S. military during World War II. As the Battle of the Bulge was raging in full fury, the worried mother went to pray at San Xavier Del Bac. It was there that the apparition of the Lady in Blue appeared and told the Native American woman that her son would be safe and survive the battle. After the war ended, the soldier did indeed return. In a way it is comforting to know that, even as the 20th century blends into the 21st, the Lady in Blue is still out there, waiting to return on a moment's notice whenever we next need her.

*Monument to the Battle of the Bulls,
the only battle fought by the Mormon
Battalion during the longest march in
military history*

chapter 40:
Battle of the Bulls

I was thrilled when I first discovered scenic Charleston Road, the shortcut between Sierra Vista and Tombstone that twists and winds through the rolling grassland hills of ranch country. When the road crossed over the Charleston bridge, spanning the flowing San Pedro River, I felt compelled to stop and enjoy the ultimate luxury in the Arizona desert – running water. My attention was caught by a small monument marker at the edge of the parking lot. Erected by a local Boy Scout troop, the monument honors the memory of the Mormon Battalion and this very spot where the soldiers claimed victory in The Battle of the Bulls. Intrigued, I knew I would have to learn more.

The Mormon Battalion was formed in 1846, a historic year for the Mormon Church and the U.S. as well. The Mormons had been forcibly evicted from their city of Nauvoo, Illinois, and were stationed at their winter quarters preparing to begin the long migration to Salt Lake and lay the foundations of the Great State of Desseret. President James K. Polk had just declared war on Mexico and troops led by Winfield Scott and Zachary Taylor would soon be marching deep into the interior of Mexico. Other troops were needed as well. Polk wanted a battalion of soldiers to march overland from New Mexico to California paving the way for future American pioneers and homesteaders. The Mormons were asked for volunteers. At first, none were willing. It took a fire and brimstone speech by the great patriarch Brigham Young to gather 500 volunteers. The soldiers were each paid seven dollars a month, a necessary sum to help pay for the migration of the church to the shores of the Great Salt Lake.

Five hundred men strong, commanded by Lieutenant Philip St. George Cooke, the Mormon Battalion departed west from Santa Fe on January 21, 1847. The battalion was guided by the legendary Arizona mountain man Pauline Weaver. At the time this region was part of the country of Mexico, but the Mormon Battalion entered what would someday become Arizona near the San Bernadino Ranch. Here they feasted on wild beef; the feral descendants of Spanish land-grant herds. The Spanish had ranched these lands for many years before fierce and frequent Apache raids had forced the ranchers to abandon their territory and leave behind thousands of head of cattle. From the San Bernadino Ranch, Weaver and Colonel Cooke led the soldiers to the San Pedro River, near where the Charleston Bridge is now located. The Mormon soldiers described the river as a picturesque and scenic refuge, much as I have found it nearly 150 years later. The foot-weary soldiers described their green and shady resting place as a pleasant stream, the banks lined with black-walnut timber and fish in abundance.

On my visits to the San Pedro I also have noticed fish in abundance, but nothing larger than minnows. Someday I hope to capture a glimpse of the reintroduced beaver that Game and Fish have released in the stream and which members of the Mormon Battalion may have been able to view as wildlife back then. Of course every time I visit the Charleston Bridge I also pay my respects to the Battle of the Bulls Monument.

The battle started on December 11, 1846, along the banks of the San Pedro River when the Mormon Battalion encountered a large herd of feral bulls. There were no cows in the herd because (the soldiers deduced) the Apaches had eaten them all. Perhaps it was the lack of female companionship that made the bulls so ornery. A group of men went hunting while the rest of the battalion marched. Two bulls were wounded by the hunters and ended up charging the marching soldiers. Sergeant Albert Smith was run over by this mini stampede and broke several of his ribs. The Mormon Battalion quickly shot the two bulls. Sergeant Smith was loaded in a wagon, and the soldiers moved out again. When they paused to water the mules down by the river, two more bulls attacked.

These bulls succeeded in upending a wagon and one of the mules was gored till the entrails hung out. The mule soon died. Still, the attack was taken lightly because it was assumed that the sound of the rifles would frighten the large and powerful beasts away. Instead the roar of the muskets only seemed to infuriate the animals. Colonel Cooke wrote, "I had to direct the men to load their muskets and defend themselves. The animals attacked without provocation."

The men pursued these two bulls, who were soon joined by a much larger group of bulls, and the Battle of the Bulls was underway amidst the roar of muskets, bellowing by both armies, and a great deal of confusion. Private Amos Cox was gored and tossed ten feet in the air, suffering wounds described as "four inches long and three inches deep." Some men climbed trees, some shot back, and others hid in the grass. Horses and mules were gored or knocked down. Lieutenant George Stoneman became so excited that he accidentally shot off his left thumb.

Expedition historian Daniel Tyler described that battle in his book History of the Mormon Battalion as follows; "The roar of musketry was heard from one end of the line to the other. One small lead mule in a team was thrown on the horns of a bull over its mate on the near side, and the near mule, now on the off side and next to the bull, was gored until he had to be left with his entrails hanging a foot below his body. Pack mules were also killed. The end gates of one or two wagons were stove in, and the sick, who were riding in them, were of course frightened. Some of the men climbed upon the wheels of the wagons and poured a deadly fire into the enemy's ranks. Some of them threw themselves down and allowed the beasts to run over them; others dodged behind mesquite brush to reload their guns, while the beasts kept them dodging to keep out of the way. Others, still, climbed up in small trees, there being now and then, one available."

The engagement with the enemy lasted several hours, the reason being that the bulls were very difficult to kill. A mad bull, Colonel Cooke noted could take, "two balls through its heart and two through its lungs and still charge man or beast." Another soldier wrote in his journal that the bulls "could run with half a dozen balls in them." The number of bulls killed in battle that day varies from account to account, ranging in number from 20 to 80. Even after all the bulls were killed and routed and the Mormon Battalion had resumed their march, one more bull came rushing out of the woods, attacked a wagon from the rear and knocked over a mule.

Levi W. Hancock, official musician of Company E, wrote a heroic ballad commemorating the historic event on the spot. The 19 stanzas of iambic quatra meter begins:

> "Under the command of Colonel Cook
> When passing down San Pedro's brook . . ."

and concludes;

> "And when the fearful fight was o'er
> And sound of muskets heard no more
> At least a score of bulls were found
> And two mules upon the ground."

The Battle of the Bulls turned out be the only combat the soldiers of the Mormon Battalion would fight during the entire Mexican War. The Mormon Battalion did succeed in capturing Tucson, Arizona. On December 15, the invading army approached the largest town in the Sonora region when a Mexican soldier rode out of the Tucson presidio to inform

Colonel Cooke that his terms of surrender had been refused. The soldier told Colonel Cooke that he should expect a fierce battle in the morning. At sunrise, the Mormon Battalion marched forward with muskets loaded and bayonets fixed. They would soon discover that the commandante of the Tucson garrison chose to flee instead of fight, taking a good portion of the Tucson population with him. The remaining citizens of Tucson welcomed the Mormon Battalion and provided them with wheat, flour, fruit, and tortillas.

From Tucson, Colonel Cooke followed the Santa Cruz River north to the Gila River. Here at Painted-Rocks-Dam State Park, visitors can see where members of the Mormon Battalion scratched their names into the rocks, rocks that are surrounded by other boulders adorned with ancient Hohokam petroglyphs. I assume that some of the soldiers were so impressed with the rock art of the Native Americans that they chose to memorialize their passage through the region by decorating the rocks themselves. The long march ended at Warner's Ranch in San Diego on January 21, 1847. Lieutenant Colonel Cooke declared proudly, "History may be searched in vain for an equal march of infantry."

Some members of the Mormon Battalion ended up in the valley of the Great Salt Lake only five days after Brigham Young had arrived. Others remained in California where a select few participated in the discovery of gold at Sutter's Mill, kicking off the California Gold Rush and the waves of 49ers. Private Amos Cox complained that the wounds he had received in the Battle of the Bulls gave him pain for the rest of his days. George Stoneman seemed to recover quite well from his self-inflicted thumb injury, going on to become the governor of California 40 years later. A great deal of territory was taken from Mexico in the war but not the part of southern Arizona that the soldiers marched through. That did not become part of the United States until the Gadsden

Purchase in 1853.

In 1858, a political dispute led to President James Buchanan ordering troops to march into Salt Lake City. The invasion was mostly a piece of political posturing as the army marched into one end of town and straight out the other side. In the meantime, at least one invading officer, Philip Saint George Cooke, paused to tip his cap in honorable salute to the patriotic members of the Mormon Battalion whom he had led on their epic march to San Diego ten years earlier.

chapter 41:
Charleston

My favorite ruin in the ghost town of Charleston used to be the one perched on the edge of the cliff overlooking the San Pedro River. It was a spectacular ruin, a single adobe wall barely clinging to the precipice atop a 50-foot-tall cliff above a slow moving bend in the river. It used to be one of my favorite ruins because a few years ago it tumbled from the cliff into the river, the victim of either erosion or vandalism. There are other ruins which stand near the edge of the cliff and many others scattered throughout the mesquite forest atop the bank. The

Adobe Ruins at Charleston

flowing river, the groves of cottonwood trees, and the colorful history of the ghost town combine to make Charleston one of the most delightful of Arizona's ghost towns.

Discovering Charleston was quite an adventure in itself. Me and my family were visiting historic Tombstone, "The town too tough to die." We were doing the tourist thing and enjoying the living history of the famous western mining boom town. Tombstone is the home of the Bird Cage Theatre, Crystal Palace Saloon, and of course the location of the infamous Shoot Out at the O.K Corral where the Earp Brothers and Doc Holliday fought members of the Clanton gang.

I was having my photograph taken in front of a sign which announced that I was standing at the exact location where the outlaw "Curly" Bill Brosious had ambushed a sheriff's deputy. While I posed for the picture an old cowboy came strolling down the Tombstone sidewalk. He was tall and lean, wearing a Stetson hat, cowboy boots, and dusty denim jeans. His skin was tan and weathered, and he looked every inch a cowboy; the real McCoy; an old timer. At least he smelled like the genuine article.

"Tourists!" the cowboy sneered as he walked past.

We walked along the wooden sidewalks and took one of the horse-drawn-wagon tours through the city streets, wandering past the historic buildings. Thirsty, we stopped for sasparilla in the Crystal Palace Saloon. Sitting down at the long bar, a country-and-western guitarist performing on stage, I looked up into the mirror and realized that the dusty, old timer was seated only a few bar stools down.

I saddled up to the bar stool next to the leathered cowboy and introduced myself. I even bought him a beer. The bartender brought the beer. The cowboy smiled and nodded. The cowboy grabbed the bottle, ignored the glass, and took a long sip.

He plopped the beer bottle down on the counter hard enough to splash some beer. "Damn Tourists!" he sneered.

And then he smiled, laughing offering me his hand to shake.

I shook his hand and then pointed out that I was no ordinary tourist. I began to recite a long litany of western historical trivia.

The cowboy shook his head, "Tourist."

"No way," and I continued my Encyclopedia of Britannica recitation.

"Simple test," the cowboy said.

"Simple test," I said, "Bring it on."

"You had your picture taken in front of the Curly Bill Brosious sign."

"Yes I did," I said proudly.

"Well then who was he?" the cowboy asked. "You had your picture taken in front of his sign – Who was Curly Bill Brosius?"

I was stunned.

"A famous outlaw." I said.

The cowboy chuckled, "You could have guessed that from the sign."

"A famous outlaw from Tombstone," I stalled.

"Wrong," the cowboy smiled. "Curly Bill Brosious lived in Charleston."

"Charleston," I said, "Where is Charleston?'

The cowboy drew us a map and we headed to the ghost town the next day.

Reaching Charleston is simple enough, take the Charleston Road cutoff between Sierra Vista and Tombstone. Follow the road from either end until you reach the double bridges crossing the San Pedro River. Park at the bridges and you will discover a small monument commemorating The Mormon Battalion and the Battle of the Bulls which was fought near here. To discover Charleston, walk north, following the railroad tracks until you come to a small train trestle. The trestle does not cross the river but provides a close view. In recent years, the BLM has put in a small wooden sign that says "Charleston" and points the direction.

Scramble down to the river and walk along the gently flowing water until you can spy some of the ruins atop the river bank. What is left of the town of Charleston is scattered atop the bluff overlooking the river.

Because of the thick mesquite forest it is difficult to view more than two or three buildings at any one time. All told there are adobe ruins of nearly 20 buildings scattered throughout the ghost town. It is somewhat eerie to walk away from one set of buildings only to stumble through the briar and bramble and suddenly come upon another set of crumbling adobe walls. Some of these abandoned structures, more than 100 years old, possess walls as high as 15-feet tall and many of the old houses have trees growing inside, branches poking out through the windows.

Charleston was founded in 1878 by Amos Stone as a byproduct of the Tombstone silver rush. Tombstone had plenty of silver but none of the water required to process the ore. As a result Charleston was born on the banks of the San Pedro River; the factories there milled tons and tons of ore. Charleston soon gained a reputation as a lawless town, especially after the losers of the gunfight at the O.K. Corral, led by old man Clanton, established a haven for outlaws. After an ambush by Mexican smugglers killed Old Man Clanton, the leadership of the desperadoes fell to Curly Bill Brosious and the notorious Johnny Ringo. It was the same Curly Bill who shot the Tombstone sheriff.

What law and order Charleston did possess was provided by the court of Judge James Burnett. Although the legitimacy of Burnett's court was in question with territorial officials, no such doubt ever existed among the citizens of Charleston. James Wolf described the judge, "He could use a .45 revolver with speed and precision. Hence there was a vast amount of order and some semblance of law in his particular vicinity at all times."

As the good citizens of Cochise County began to clamor for a more civilized society, activities such as smuggling, rustling, and robbery were removed as pillars of the Charleston economy. To show just how civilized they had become, the mill owner at Charleston hired a small orchestra to play at an important social occasion. Although based out of nearby Bisbee, many of the musicians were from Texas. A heated debate soon turned into a battle of fisticuffs as the musicians and the audience argued over whether Arizona or Texas was better, men wildly swinging violins during the fight.

When the Tombstone mines flooded in 1886, the Charleston silver mills were shut down and the town soon followed. The legendary Johnny Ringo eventually shot himself, an opium addict and suicide victim. The subject is a matter of some historical controversy because some experts claim that Johnny Ringo was really murdered and robbed by a two bit gambler known as Johnny Behind the Deuce. In 1888 the post office was closed and in 1889 the last miners and outlaws abandoned the town. Legend has it that, before they left, the last rowdy residents of the renegade town nailed an atlas of Arizona to a post, formed a firing squad and blew Charleston off the map.

Today, you can sit on the banks of the San Pedro River and watch the buildings as they gradually tumble from the eroding cliffs or you can wander the mesquite bosques where the crumbling adobe ruins appear in clusters and wonder if remains of the building before you used to be a church, bank, Chinese grocer, miners cabin, or even home to one of the west's more legendary outlaws. I stand near the edge of the cliff overlooking the river. When a family member approaches he startles an owl from a tree.

The owl explodes from amidst the mesquite thicket, launching itself from the cliff. The big fluffy, feathery body sails the open sky above the river before landing in the autumn leaves among the thick groves of cottonwood trees on the far bank.

We return to Tombstone that evening, stopping for another sasparilla at the Crystal Palace Saloon. Looking into the reflection in the long mirror behind the bar, I see the old timer enter. I buy him a beer and thank him for pointing me toward Charleston. He nods and smiles.

"Whatever happened to Curly Bill Brosious?" I ask.

"He and his gang used to run into Mexico and rob the train. They say that some of his gang left a treasure buried at the mouth of Skeleton canyon, close to where Geronimo surrendered. Curly Bill participated in the ambush and murder of Morgan Earp and eventually Wyatt Earp caught up to him. Wyatt ambushed Curly Bill in the Whetstone Mountains and shot him in his sleeping roll, blasting him in the face at point blank range.

"Well thanks again," I say, "Charleston was beautiful."

A newcomer jumps into the conversation, a few bar stools down. "Me and my friends fly ultralight aircraft and this morning we flew low over the San Pedro River. There was no doubt where Charleston was located, the adobe walls are very visible from the air. Besides, you can see all these holes left behind by treasure hunters seeking buried outlaw treasure."

The old timer smiled. "Back in the days before Charleston was a protected archaeological site, I discovered this." He reached into his pocket, retrieving his wallet. He unfolded the battered, beaten, leather and produced a small object wrapped in tissue paper. Carefully, he unfolded the tissue paper.

Inside was a small coin, a silver five-centavos piece, dating back to 1878. The coin still wears the mark of a fierce eagle on the obverse and back in those days, the coin would have been made of real silver.

"Yep," the old cowboy smiled, "Nowadays it would be illegal to pick up that coin but back when I was a boy it was fine. And who knows, maybe even Curly Bill Brosious himself spent this coin after acquiring it illegally in a Mexican robbery."

The only treasure I found that day was a feather that fell off a frightened owl. Well, an owl feather, an adventure, and the ghost of Curly Bill Brosious.

chapter 42:
Apache Bears

In Arizona, the bears live atop the mountain peaks, high above the desert floor. The bruins seek sanctuary from the summer sun atop their sky-island ceilings, hidden in their boulder fortresses. The Apache have long believed that if you were a good warrior in this life, you came back in the next life as a bear.

One of the initiation rites of a young Apache brave was to head into the mountains with only a loincloth and a spear. The battle between the skinny teenager and the mighty bear was a lot more evenly matched than most hunting expeditions. Needless to say, many young men never returned from such a quest. A young man who did come back carrying a bear pelt over his shoulder was probably well on his way towards becoming a fearsome warrior.

Cochise may have been the greatest warrior the Apache have ever known. While he was alive, all the residents of southeastern Arizona feared his wrath. Cochise became known as a powerful leader among the Apache after the murder of his father in law, Mangas Coloradas, at the hands of some soldier prospectors. Cochise led his marauding warriors on the bloody path of vengeance. He nearly succeeded in depopulating the region of settlers.

Whenever soldiers followed Cochise, he and his warriors would retreat into the heart of the Dragoon Mountains; an impenetrable fortress of stone known as Cochise's Stronghold. Cochise died a free man, without ever being subjugated by the government of the United States. Cochise did not consider himself to be a warrior by profession but rather a victim of circumstance. The most famous of the stories about Cochise involve his negotiations for peace.

Tom Jeffords was a mail superintendent, in charge of running the mail through the middle of the Apache country. As a wagon driver he had been wounded by Apache arrows many times. Jeffords was responsible for hiring men who were willing to risk the dangerous job of driving the mail for a salary of $125 a month. Jeffords rarely had to pay as very few drivers lasted an entire month. Jeffords felt guilty about sending man after man to his death. They were usually teen-aged orphans. He decided to do something about the situation.

Jeffords rode into the mountains alone and unarmed, wandering lost for three days. Perhaps amused, the Apache scouts did not ambush and kill the solitary white man. Instead, they took him to meet Cochise.

"I have come to see you as a friend," Jeffords stated. "I hear that you are an honest man."

"I am." Cochise said.

"I speak only for myself," Jeffords declared. "I want peace with you. I do not want your men to kill my men."

Cochise was touched by the white man who risked his own life to save the lives of others. Cochise made a request in return. Cochise agreed to sign a peace treaty only if Jeffords was appointed reservation agent.

The surprised Jeffords reluctantly agreed. All that remained was the formal singing of the treaty. General O. O. Howard and several of his highest ranking officers made the journey into the heart of the Dragoon Mountains to negotiate with Cochise. The American soldiers were understandably nervous, outnumbered, and surrounded by hundreds of Apache warriors.

The Apache peoples were genuinely interested in peace. They provided a bountiful feast with lots of venison, quail,

Black bear in the Chirachaua Mountains

roasted corn and mesquite beans. The Apache musicians played their three-stringed fiddles while the soldiers and Native Americans danced all night long. Plenty of *tiswin* (or corn beer) was provided for everybody.

Now it was the turn of Cochise and his men to spend a night at Fort Bowie. Fort Bowie was located near a place the Americans called Apache Pass. The Spanish referred to it as The Door of the Dice because of the risk involved in journeying through the Apache countryside. Inside the walls of Fort Bowie, it was Cochise and his men who were now outnumbered and surrounded. Like the Apache, the soldiers desired peace and did their best to be generous hosts. The Americans served up beef and lamb, chicken, eggs and brandy. One of the soldiers grabbed his fiddle and the people danced in celebration.

When the festivities came to an end and it became time for slumber, General Howard offered his best bear skin rugs to the Apache soldiers as bedding. The Apache warriors looked at Cochise in terror. How could they sleep inside the skins of former warriors? Many of them grabbed for their weapons.

"See, I told you it was a trick," one of the warriors exclaimed, "The white sorcerers want to wrap us in ghosts."

Cochise was able to calm his men and the peace was preserved, at least temporarily. That night, Howard wrote in his journal, "These Apache, I will never understand them. They reject my bear skin rugs and they choose to shiver all night long on the cold, hard floor."

He never did understand.

The peace lasted until the Mickey Free incident.

Mickey Free was a child who lived near Sonoita. A band of Pinaleno Apache massacred a homestead and kidnapped the boy. An officer from the local cavalry post blamed Cochise for the crime. Cochise protested his innocence and even offered his assistance in capturing the kidnappers. The officer refused and had Cochise arrested. The Apache chieftain and a hand full of followers were shackled and led inside a tent. Cochise quickly undid his bonds and untied his friends. They slipped out the back of the tent and Cochise returned to the war path.

Cochise was never defeated. He died a free man. On his death bed, he asked for one last visit from his friend Tom Jeffords. He and Jeffords made a promise to visit each other in the afterworld. Cochise died and was buried somewhere in the stronghold. Hundreds of horses were ridden across the mesa in every direction to obscure Cochise's last resting place.

I like to think that maybe Cochise isn't resting, that somewhere in the Chiricahua Mountains a black bear roams the rugged mountain slopes while daydreaming of the past when he used to be an Apache warrior, riding the grasslands of southern Arizona atop the fastest horse anyone had ever seen.

chapter 43:
Ventana Cave

Ventana is the Spanish word for window, a reference to the beautiful rock arch visible on the far horizon. I have never seen it photographed in any newspaper or journal. Part of the reason must be the rugged isolation that hides both the arch and the cave named after it.

Ventana Cave is located in the very heart of the Tohono O'odham Reservation. The O'odham have another name for this ancient cave. Speaking barely above a whisper, the O'odham elders call this place The House of Whirlwinds.

Two of Arizona's most renowned archaeologists, Emil Haury and Julian Hayden, led the excavations at Ventana Cave in 1941 and 1942. The archaeology crew consisted of graduate students and many local O'odham. Two of the O'odham, a pair of respected elders, went to another nearby cave called the House of Lightning. They performed an ancient ceremony and asked permission of the Ventana ghosts to excavate their remains. The O'odham have never allowed an excavation of the House of Lightning.

Dr. Haury reported that, once they had been given permission, as soon as they began to dig, a small dust devil started to spin in the back of the cave, careening between the boulders and the cave paintings. Haury said the dust devil traveled the entire length of the rock overhang, growing in size until it was as large as a human being. Then it spun in one place at the far end of the cavern, twirling feverishly until it burned itself out.

Dr. Haury rushed over to where the whirling dervish had expired and realized that the dust devil had exposed a big toe. An entire skeleton was eventually revealed and unearthed, a skeleton belonging to an ancient shaman buried with seashell jewelry and a heron bone rattle.

Ventana Cave was first inhabited approximately 10,000 years ago and was continuously inhabited until 1400 AD. This period covers civilizations from the spear-toting big-game hunters of the receding Ice Age, to the rise, flowering, and collapse of the Hohokam, and the arrival of the O'odham culture.

Fossil remains of Pleistocene mammals included dire wolf, giant bison, four-pronged antelope, and jaguar. Extinct species of tapir, horse, and giant-ground sloth were found in the lowest levels of the cave stratigraphy, along with the projectile points of the people who hunted them.

The Chiricahua-Amargosa culture left behind sandals, woven clothes, and stone tools for processing plant foods. The Hohokam came next, leaving behind pottery shards and corn cobs. The Hohokam were a scientific theocracy, a combination of wizards and astronomer priests who made the desert bloom. The Papago people or Tohono O'odham as they prefer to be known, are the people who still live on these lands with roots going all the way into the back of the cave and deep into the heart of the mountain itself.

The hike to Ventana Cave requires a short, steep climb up a narrow, winding path. As I approach the precipice, the cave comes alive with chattering and an explosion of feathers. Hundreds of quail flee my footsteps. So many tiny, chubby birds fly up at once that it takes four or five minutes before the sky can hold them all.

Stepping beneath the rock overhang it is obvious at once why the quail seek sanctuary here. The rock ceiling provides shade from the burning sun. The back of the cave holds a pool of water from an underground spring. The rock ceiling is adorned with *pictographs*; Native American rock art that dates back thousands of years. My favorite is a bear paw which uses a dark stain in the rock as the center of the paw and then outlines the foot and claws in red.

Hayden and Haury dug in the soft dirt, discovering layers of history buried in Ventana Cave. It developed an amazing timeline for the cultures which have risen, thrived, and decayed in the southwest. The archaeology work was seasonal; depending on academic schedules, grant money, and the weather. As the dig progressed, two O'odham elders

Bear paw pictograph

were amazed by the secrets of their ancestors being unearthed. They were also saddened by how much information had been lost and allowed to perish.

The elders resolved to keep at least one ceremony alive. It was a ceremony specific to the House of Lightning. A small gathering of men arrived at the hidden cave one night, trying to revive the ancient magic. They armed themselves with sage, eagle feathers, and thunder sticks. How loudly the thunder sticks must have echoed as they boomed inside the cavern, while the drummers beat and the singers sang.

The piercing whistle of the bone flutes punctured the air with shrieking percussive accents. Yet, when the powerful ritual had ended, the elders sighed. There were no young people here to keep the magic alive. There were only elders in attendance. The ceremony was in danger of disappearing.

The thoughts of the elders were interrupted by the coughing of a mountain lion. The lion wished to seek refuge in the Cave of Lightning. Finding it occupied, it unleashed a mighty roar. The elders left the cave as quickly as possible.

The mountain lion entered the cave, coughed, lay down and slowly died.

Julian Hayden liked to tell the story of the day he was digging in the back of the cave with a trowel in his hand when a miniature dust devil started just beyond the edge of his fingertips. At first, the tiny whirlwind was no bigger than his finger but as it spun and spun it quickly grew larger, becoming as big as Hayden's fist and then his head. The dust devil moved quickly, twirling between the boulders and stones, dancing wildly beneath the cave paintings. Suddenly it leapt from the precipice and stretched to twice its size. As the dust devil tore up the cactus it continued growing in strength and in whirling frenzy.

By the time it reached the archaeologist's camp it was huge and tossed tents, cooking gear, notebooks, and sleeping bags all across the desert. By the time it had reached the Santa Rosa Mountains across the valley the whirlwind was taller than the peaks themselves. The camp was so thoroughly destroyed that the archaeologists were forced to return to Tucson.

Many decades later, Julian Hayden braved a return to Ventana Cave and the House of Whirlwinds. While he was there, he even stole a peek at the cave the elders call the House of Lightning. There amidst the bat guano was a mountain lion skeleton. The ceremony had never been revived and Hayden was forced to wonder if perhaps the magic had been forgotten.

Hidden deep inside the Tohono O'odham nation there are still many hidden secrets just waiting to be discovered, but I think intrepid explorers must be very cautious when they open the door to the House of Whirlwinds.

Jios at o m-we:majik (Be with God).

chapter 44:
Rillito Roadside Shrine

I take my eye away from the automobile temperature gauge, look up at the road, and spot the roadside shrine. My car is overheating and we have been tooling along frontage roads and back alleyways for miles trying to nurse it home. While amidst the ruins of a Hohokam village photographing petroglyphs, a radiator hose sprung a leak. Now my desperate journey has taken me to this unexpected site. I stop the car beside the roadside shrine. I can kill two birds with one stone, adding water to the radiator and using the last few photographs inside my roll of film.

I pop the automobile hood and loosen the cap, causing clouds of steam to rise up into the air. With camera in hand, I begin photographing the shrine. Like many roadside shrines in Arizona, a small religious statue is housed inside a small half-dome structure. This shrine is built of stone and mortar and is a little larger than most. The statue inside is about three feet tall and made of concrete. The religious statue has a homemade feel, sincerely but simply crafted, a bald man wearing brown robes, a cape and crucifix draped over his shoulders. There are flowers at the base of the statue, both real and perfumed. The saint is surrounded by small ceramic-animal statues; rabbits, cows, and birds.

It is these animals which identify the statue as representing St. Francis of Assisi. Francis was the vagabonding son of a wealthy man who took a vow of poverty and dedicated his life to serving God. Saint Francis recognized that all living things were loved equally by God; including Brother Fire and Sister Death. Saint Francis was famous for preaching sermons to birds and, according to legends, once convinced a wolf to stop devouring humans. In 1979 Pope John Paul II declared Saint Francis de Assisi patron of the ecology movement.

There is a painting by Apache artist Jim Stevens in a church on the Maricopa Ak-Chin reservation which depicts Saint Francis preaching to the desert animals. Listening in the foreground are quail, roadrunner, cactus wren, tortoise, coyote, and Gila monster. Approaching in the background are a pair of horses; animals that were introduced after the arrival of the Spanish. When the Jesuits were expelled from New Spain it was Franciscan missionaries, the order founded and named after Saint Francis, who flocked to the new world preaching the gospel in the arid deserts of the southwest.

My automobile has stopped hissing like a steam demon and I approach it cautiously. With a rag in my hand, I remove the radiator cap. A large canteen empties into the radiator as a small vapor of melted water rises skyward. If vultures could devour metal they would be circling above my car.

Folklorist "Big" Jim Griffith tells a tale involving three saints in one – the story of Saint Francis or San Francisco, informal patron-saint of the southwestern deserts. The story begins with the energetic, exploring Jesuit missionary, Father Eusebio Francisco Kino, who traveled thousands of miles, built scores of churches and mapped everything in sight. It was Father Kino who founded the mission at San Xavier del Bac, the beautiful church south of Tucson known as The White Dove of the Desert. When he died at Magdalena (his bones are buried beneath the church), Father Kino was on his way to San Xavier with a statue of Saint Francis of Xavier.

Saint Francis of Xavier was among the first of the Jesuit missionaries to be martyred. Saint Francis of Xavier was Father Kino's personal patron saint and the good priest wished to honor him with a statue for the southern Arizona church which bore his name. The mule which Father Kino used to bring the statue of Saint Francis of Xavier to

Magdalena refused to move any further from the beautiful Mexican city. According to legends, Father Kino pulled and tugged on the stubborn mule so hard that he had a heart attack and died. Father Kino's bones are buried on the spot. The statue remains inside the Magdalena church to this day.

Every year on October 4th, the feast day of Saint Francis of Assisi, tens of thousands of pilgrims head to Magdalena. They come from every direction, especially from among the Native Americans; Yaqui, Mayo, Opata, and especially the O'odham. Tohono O'odham from both sides of the border; Arizona and Sonora, flock to Magdalena for the religious fiesta. The history of the church at San Xavier in the 20th century involves a long line of priests trying to convince the O'odham pilgrims to stay home. But every year on October 4th the roads to Magdalena are packed and the crowds enjoy the religious festival; food, family, friends, musicians, and vendors.

As the Spanish presence on their northern frontier waned, the gospel they had spread became more and more interpreted through the eyes of Native Americans. The final result was the creation of the Sonoran Folk Catholic Church and a religious holiday where three saints are rolled into one.

To many of the Native Americans visiting Magdalena, the feast day of Saint Francis of Assisi, the statue of Saint Francis of Xavier, and the bones of Father Eusebio Francisco Kino buried there, all belong to the same man, a sort of ubiquitous San Francisco who is the informal patron saint of the southwest.

I place the radiator cap back on and close the hood to my automobile. I offer the religious statue a salute, wondering if he is one of these three in one saints. Certainly, the people who leave flowers, candles, and pictures of loved ones, believe in this statue with all their hearts. This particular roadside shrine is located along an interstate frontage road, with railroad tracks behind. The cars roll past at high rates of speed, the big trucks leaving behind a gust of wind. The closest town is Rillito.

The tiny and recent town of Rillito, Arizona, has an interesting history. The town of Rillito was founded in the 1950s. In the years following World War II, many African Americans made their living by working across the southwest as migrant agricultural labor. They would pick cotton in Phoenix and citrus in Tucson. Many of these men were from Texas or the deep south. Most of these migrant workers were desperate, attempting to escape the sharecropping lifestyle of their parents.

There was one man from Texas who discovered that out near Tangerine Road land was for sale – cheap! The owner lived back east and he did not care what color the skin of the buyer was, as long as the money was green. Opportunities for black men to buy land in the 1950s were few and far between. As word spread between friends and family members, more and more of these migrant workers purchased land in the area until at last they were able stop their wandering and establish a home in a community they named Rillito.

I drop to one knee and look underneath the car. Some of the water I poured into the radiator is already starting to drip out. I also spy, lying on the ground just behind the car, a wool blanket. I get up and inspect the blanket. It is a good thick heavy wool blanket, dyed bright colors. It is the type of wool blanket which you only find in rural communities, the kind where sheep are raised. The ground is also littered with plastic bottles, hats, canteens, and scraps of clothing. My traveling companion has a theory, "It looks like maybe they busted a bunch of illegal aliens here. Like a bunch of objects you would take on a long journey were suddenly discarded."

I can picture the hypothetical scene clearly. A van pulled over by a siren and flashing lights. Uniformed officers slide open the door and a small group of men pile out from the vehicle, hands on their heads. More and more men pile from the van, more people than you would have believed could have possibly fit inside the vehicle. They speak rapidly to each other in Spanish while the uniformed men bark loud orders in both Spanish and English.

The men of the Border Patrol work briskly, efficiently, trying to keep order at the scene, aware that today, tomorrow, or maybe two years down the road will come the violent confrontation that can end their life, the life of their partner, or perhaps force them to kill someone else. Some of the Mexican men, men filling the same economic niche once occupied by the African Americans who pioneered Rillito, nervously drop some of their belongings, a hat or a wool blanket. It is easy to picture one of the illegals offering a prayer to the statue of San Francisco just before he is arrested and loaded into a government vehicle.

I grab the wool blanket and place it in my overheating vehicle, turn the key and nurse the car home. It was a bad decision. Of course, hindsight is 20-20, but looking back I probably should have stuck out my thumb and taken my chances with hitchhiking. By the time I reached my home town, my car engine was making a knock, knock, knocking sound. The car had gotten so hot that the distributor cap had begun to melt. My car was very, very dead.

Some months after that I began having trouble sleeping. I would wake up in the middle of the night and lie there. At first I thought it was just money worries. The grind of a new car payment was wearing down my budget. Then I realized it was more. The statue of Saint Francis in the Rillito Roadside shrine began to appear in my dreams. Not the whole statue, just his head, floating in my dreams.

Sometimes he would laugh and laugh, then I would wake up in a cold sweat, stare at the clock, and lay awake until it was time to go to work. I was missing something.

The image of the head of the roadside shrine statue haunted me for weeks. I could not quite place it. In the meantime I kept on doing those things that take up so much of everyday life; family, work, friends, and worry about bills. It was quite awhile before I could afford to develop the photographs from the

St. Francis statue at the Rillito roadside (head not original)

petroglyph adventure which had introduced me to the Rillito roadside shrine and killed my car. By that time I had a collection of six rolls of film from various escapades. It wasn't until I developed the photographs and saw the bald visage of Saint Francisco smiling at me, just like in my dreams, that I realized where I had seen it before. It was in a book.

I had seen a photograph of the Rillito roadside shrine somewhere in a book. Which book? I tore apart my library, frantically flipping pages. One messy living room later I discovered a photograph of Saint Francis on the inside of a book jacket. In that photograph, San Francisco is wearing a different cape. The book is Jim Griffith's *Saints of the Southwest*. Big Jim describes the Rillito roadside shrine as having been built in the 1940s. He also informs me that the head now on the statue is not the original one, the first one being stolen by vandals many decades ago. Who would steal a cement saint's head from a religious statue?

I decide to make a pilgrimage back to the roadside shrine in my new car. I bring a candle and light it. I light some of the other candles already there as well. I pick some of the nearby wildflowers, poppies and blue lupine, and leave them at the base of statue. I leave some change and a couple of bills, enough for a bite to eat in case a vagabond traveler should ever happen by.

Oh, and the wool blanket, it sat in my closet and led a useless life until the other day when my cat had four kittens on it. Four black-and-white, cute-as-a-button kittens, kept warm by a hastily discarded blanket. I have to believe Saint Francis would have been pleased.

Jim Huntington, former
editor of The Oracle
September 7, 1943 - August 14, 2003

chapter 45:
Mount Graham Sacred Run

I did not expect to write this article. I had heard of the sacred run on the radio news but did not know much about it. Coming home from work one day, I cursed the unusual traffic congestion on American Avenue in the tiny town of Oracle. There were vans pulled alongside the road, edging on to the pavement. The vans were filled with people. "Probably tourists," I muttered under my breath.

I could not have been more wrong. As I neared the front of the parked cars I came upon a pair of young Native American men running along the road. One held a wooden staff adorned with eagle feathers high above his head. The wind blew his long hair and eagle feathers behind him, trailing like a celestial tail. I realized that I had stumbled upon the sacred run of the Apache.

Known officially as the Mount Graham Sacred Run, the annual relay-style run was started by a group calling themselves The Spirit of the Mountain Relay Runners. The first run ten years ago was meant to protest and prevent the construction of telescopes atop a sacred mountain. The first of the Mount Graham telescopes was completed a long time ago. The run has endured however.

"You can't subtract the telescopes from this. But something bad, the telescopes, has woken up what is good." said run organizer Wendsler Nosie Sr., a Chiricahua Apache. "This run has changed a lot of lives. People have been touched. There are personal things people find very spiritual and different people are affected in different ways."

I drive down American Avenue to the post office and pick up my mail. When I double back towards home I pass the Sacred Run again. There is quite the automobile caravan supporting the runners. People with cameras line the road, Native Americans, local residents, journalists, and curious onlookers. I drive slowly, cautiously. The runners appear around a bend in the road. The relay has changed hands. Now a middle-aged married couple carries the sacred staff, eagle feathers blowing in the breeze. They huff and puff. They do not allow their exertion to show in their pace, running proud.

As a protest, the Mount Graham Sacred Run has been remarkably ineffective. Two Mount Graham telescopes were operational by 1994. The large binocular telescope went into operation in 2004 and four more telescopes are being planned. Recently there was a victory when the mountain top was listed with the National Register of Historic Places as traditional cultural property of Western Apache tribes.

The run has grown every year with more and more participants. The 2003 run included Cibecue Apache, San Carlos Apache, White Mountain Apache, Lakota, Akimel O'odham, Tohono O'odham, Navajo, Yaqui from both the American and Mexican sides of the border, as well as the Tarahumara from deep in the heart of Mexico's rugged Sierra Madre Mountains. There were supporters from France, Algeria, Denmark. North Carolina, New York, and Italy. Some of the supporters from Italy were here to protest the role of the Vatican in the Mount Graham telescopes.

Many of the people in Oracle became instant supporters, coming out to cheer, clap, or wave as they drove past real slow. Wendsler Nosie Sr. was right. There is something about this run which touches people. All day there was a pulsing charge racing through Oracle. I overhead people at the post office and store talking, "Did you see the sacred runners?" The topic of conversation put a smile on people's faces

Each runner in the relay must carry a sacred staff that has

been decorated and blessed. The ceremonies began with two nights of sweat lodges on the Apache reservation. On July 31st the runners set out from the Pascua Yaqui reservation inside the city of Tucson. They set a brisk pace for their eventual goal to reach the top of Mount Graham. This run of more than 100 miles contains a lot of uphill areas and takes two full days.

I stumbled upon the runners as they passed through Oracle on the first day of the run. The runners were making good time, still needing to cover quite a bit of ground before they made camp for the night in Aravaipa Canyon. This year there was a memorial service for the approximately 170 Aravaipa Apache who were slaughtered in the Camp Grant Massacre

In an open dirt lot along American Avenue I noticed several vehicles. Someone had set a up a ramada with cloth canopy fluttering in the wind. Impulsively, I pulled into the parking lot to observe the scene. It was quite the nomadic automotive tribe; there were trucks, RVs, government vans, and tiny little economy cars. In keeping with the best of the nomadic traditions there was even a truck pulling a tiny trailer dragging a port-a-potty.

The lot was filled with people, many of them Native American, others not. One young boy wore a turkey feather in his hat, riding in the back of a pickup truck as it led the runners. Many of those in attendance wore T-shirts which proudly proclaimed tribal affiliations. One beautiful young woman wore an "I Love NY" cap. Some of the vans were filled with rows of rugged, athletic looking young men who looked like they could run very quickly.

Underneath the cloth ramada there was a table laden with grapes, fruit and lots of water. There were also two very large ironwood sculptures of Yaqui deer dancers. The next runner was preparing himself. He looked fit, like he ran on a regular basis; far and fast. He was probably a good choice to carry the staff along the steep rolling hills out of Oracle. There were many people at the ramada with cameras and video recorders.

One of those people with a camera was my friend J.C. Huntington. He was also my boss because he was the publisher of our local newspaper. Both of us had published articles in the newspaper about Buffalo Bill Cody. It gave us something to talk about whenever we crossed paths. This particular day when we crossed paths at the Sacred Run, he was particularly exuberant. With camera in hand, he was taking photographs and wearing a great big smile. He was talking to everybody, asking questions, and taking mental notes as fast as he could think, trying to absorb everything.

Like me, J.C. had bumped into the Sacred Run without expecting it. Both of us had been compelled by curiosity to stop in and learn. We compared notes. J.C. was planning on writing an article, so I didn't need to. People began to line American Avenue again and we took our places to cheer the runner on. As the young man who looked so fast finished his final stretching exercises, J.C. suddenly jumped in his truck and said he was going to drive down the road and get better photographs. I wished him well and told him I looked forward to reading the article he was going to write. Little did I realize that it would be the last time I ever saw him.

The Spirit of The Mountain Runners held a ceremony atop Mount Graham on August 3rd, 2003. The sacred staff was placed in a secret location, alongside nine other staffs from the previous years. Next year sacred staff number 11 will be added to the pile. The run has become a form of bonding for families; parents, children, and married couples, and strengthens friendships between different nations. Hopefully, next year's run will be even bigger and pass through Oracle again.

On August 15th, 2003, a wall of whitewater flash flood came roaring down Campo Bonito and took the life of J.C. Huntington, the publisher of *The Oracle* monthly newspaper. The tragedy hurt me personally and the community experienced an irreplaceable loss. In an interview, Dean Prichard was quoted as saying that JC Huntington was probably in the middle of the wash taking photos of the flood when it overran him.

I could not help but wonder if the camera still held the shots of the sacred runners or if he had already gotten them developed. We will miss you dearly J.C. but I will always treasure the last time I saw you at the Mount Graham Sacred Run. You were so exuberant that you glowed, running around asking questions and taking pictures. Like your publishing career, The Sacred Run is an environmental battle cry. Like your vision for *The Oracle*, the Mount Graham Sacred Run is all about building community, strengthening bonds between people. Like the organizers of the Sacred Run, you never allowed setbacks to dismay you, always continuing the fight and expecting victory simply because our hearts are true and our cause is just.

I never expected to write this article but tragic events led me to put word to paper, I just wanted to say how glad I am that the last time I saw you, you were happy and enthusiastically engaged in an activity meant to celebrate life, meant to praise the earth. The last time I saw you, you were trying to make the world a better place. Sounds just like you.

Macho B

courtesy of Arizona Game and Fish Department

chapter 46:
Macho B, Most Famous Jaguar in the World

On March 7th 1996 in the Pelconcillo Mountains near the New Mexico border with both Arizona and Mexico, rancher Warner Glenn was hunting with his dogs when "I thought the dogs had treed a lion but when I went to look, it was a jaguar." Mr. Glenn ran to his saddlebag, reached for his holster . . . and removed his camera. Warner Glenn's pictures of the jaguar, included in his book titled *Eyes of Fire* were the first photographs of a live jaguar ever taken in the United States.

From that moment forward, his life was changed and Warner Glenn dedicated his life to jaguar conservation. Glenn helped conservation groups place video cameras in the mountains hoping to capture more images of these elusive beasts. Unfortunately four of the cameras were quickly stolen, presumably by drug smugglers. Images of jaguars on different video cameras, this time placed along the Arizona/ Mexico border, appeared soon enough. Beginning in the late 1990s, cameras have captured 69 photographs, five video clips, and 28 sets of tracks belonging to several different jaguars.

The border cameras intended to photograph jaguars were wildly successful, probably none more so than the cameras set up by Jack Childs in the mountains of southern Arizona, mostly the Patagonia and Baboquivari ranges. First a beautiful male cat they named *Macho A* was captured in the camera lens in 2001. Then the camera photographed a second male, a majestic jaguar who was called *Macho B*. Macho B soon became the most photographed wild jaguar in the world, seen through the lens dozens of times for almost a decade. Macho B was a big beautiful jaguar estimated to weigh about 150 pounds and grew to be at least 13 or 15 years old. He was photographed at different locations many times over many years, including a wonderful videotape in the Santa Rita Mountains, and yet when we add up the sum total of all the pictures, we realize they are nothing more than glimpses of a shadow slipping in and out of our mountain ranges. We already know Macho B was a longtime resident of the United States and wandered over a lot of country but have very few details to fill in the story. Although Macho B and other jaguars travel great distances, and must cross civilization's path frequently, they are rarely seen, spotted ghosts passing by silently.

Since government regulations declared there were no jaguars in Arizona there was debate about whether it was illegal to shoot one. Once the border cameras confirmed that jaguars did indeed live here, a much more heated debate followed on whether we should protect a large predator known to stalk human beings. Jaguars were eventually given status as an endangered species; but today many conservation groups are frustrated with the pace of government protection. A group called Defenders of Wildlife recently filed suit protesting the delay of a federal protection plan for the jaguar. This suit is expected to be joined with a similar suit filed in 2007 by the Center of Biological Diversity. In particular, environmentalists are upset about the possible effects of a border fence interfering with the voluntary migration of jaguars from Mexico into the United States, as well as make it difficult for jaguars already residing in the United States to cross back and forth freely.

U.S. Fish and Wildlife called the American jaguar a "foreign species" that cannot be recovered in the United States. Fish and Wildlife declares, "The United States supports a small fraction of the individuals and available habitat for the jaguar." Michael Robinson of the Center for Biological Diversity rebuts, "If having few individuals in the

U.S. disqualifies an endangered species from a recovery plan, gray wolves would have never been reintroduced ... (Jaguar) numbers exceed the number of wolves known in the Rocky Mountains or the southwest when recovery plans were adopted for them."

February 20, 2008, Warner Glenn, the first man to photograph a wild jaguar in the United States, had a second wild jaguar encounter in the Animas Mountains of New Mexico. A hunting dog named Powder returned to camp with a huge hole in his neck and shoulder. Glenn said, "Something had pounded the pudding out of Powder." Five other hunting dogs picked up the scent and Warner Glenn followed as fast as he could manage. When he got within 500 yards of the commotion, "I looked up and in the shade of a big cedar tree I could see a big cat. I thought they'd have a big tom lion. I moved in closer. The cat charged the dogs. They scattered like quail. Then I saw it was a jaguar."

Mr. Glenn grabbed his camera and started shooting. The jaguar caught a dog named Copper, bit him on the back and released him. In a *New York Times* interview, Glenn said, "The jaguar could have easily killed the dogs, one bite to the head and they'd be gone. He let them go on purpose."

When the rest of the hunting party arrived, the jaguar stared them in the eyes before trotting away slowly with confidence. "He did not run," Glenn said. "He was not afraid of anything." Witnesses estimated the cat was eight or nine years old and nearly 200 pounds. Glenn named the big jaguar *Border King*.

On November 14, 2008 a wild born jaguar arrived at the Phoenix Zoo. This special cat is the only jaguar born in the wild on display at any zoo in North America. It took years of planning for this jaguar named *Lucero* to travel from Sonora, Mexico to Arizona. This young male will call the Phoenix

Zoo home for at least a year. The Arizona Game and Fish Department orchestrated the loan as a way to provide medical aid to the jaguar. Lucero had been illegally captured and kept in an inadequate enclosure where the giant feline damaged its canine teeth. The Phoenix Zoo agreed to provide the necessary dental assistance. After the giant cat was sedated, X-rays and blood samples were taken which revealed extensive damage. Veterinarians extracted upper incisors and performed four root canals on the other affected teeth. Dr. Chris Visser, a board certified veterinary dental specialist volunteered his time to perform the surgery. Phoenix Zoo president Bert Castro said, "We are grateful that Dr. Visser's work will improve the quality of life of this jaguar and we hope to learn more about this magnificent animal. After its stay in quarantine, this amazing animal will be on exhibit so that our guests can meet it and learn more about the plight of the jaguar in this region."

What zoo guests will learn is that at one time the American jaguar roamed from Monterey Bay to the Appalachian Mountains, from the Grand Canyon deep into South America. Jaguars are not only the largest wild cats in North America but they are the only wild cats in the Americas who can roar. Jaguars eat deer, javelina, eggs, birds, rodents, reptiles, and are rumored to devour the occasional human. Their preferred habitats include grasslands, thickly forested riparian zone, and the most rugged, remote, inaccessible regions of southwestern wilderness.

During Lucero's stay in the Phoenix Zoo, biologists will be conducting DNA studies on the jaguar so they can look for differences between the northern jaguar population and the populations found in Central and South America. The cooperation between Game and Fish and the Mexican government is part of a tradition of working together for over 20 years, already reintroducing such animals as whooping cranes, Gould's turkey, Yaqui fish, desert pupfish, and an expanded population of Sonoran pronghorn. Now that he has healed from the dental surgery, Lucero the jaguar will be proudly displayed at the Phoenix Zoo where zoo goers can observe the magnificent jungle cat with the bright shiny smile.

That bright shiny smile has already worked its magic. Lucero has a new girlfriend. Shortly before Lucero's arrival at the Phoenix Zoo, the zoo serendipitously welcomed the arrival of a zoo born female from Florida. *Caciora* is a cute kittenish jaguar of Brazilian ancestry. As soon as Lucero was brought into the enclosure beside her, Caciora pressed her nose to the fence, stomped her paws and wagged her tail. She wanted to make friends with the handsome new boy in town. Lucero seemed more perplexed by his new surroundings than in returning the attentions of his new female admirer. I have been to the Phoenix Zoo recently and Caciora is very cute. I am certain her graceful prancing will soon win Lucero's heart.

I was conversing with one zoo official who groaned at the amount of bureaucratic paperwork that would be the result of these two giant cats consummating their love. He claims proper paperwork, with all the "i"s dotted and all the "t"s crossed, will need to be filed with seventeen different agencies spread across two governments before these two amorous jaguars can do something that would happen quite spontaneously and naturally in the wild.

If the two jaguars do receive the bureaucratic stamp of approval for their romance it will represent a melding of the northern and southern jaguar populations, the same populations biologists are studying to ascertain subtle differences. Staring at the two jaguars in their side-by-side enclosures, there are a few visible differences. She is more of a bright yellow where he is more of a dusty orange to blend in better with his desert environment. The camouflage coats of both cats work remarkably well. When either cat is still and motionless, the viewer is forced to survey the enclosure just to earn a glimpse of cat. I stand on the edge of Caciora's cage, knowing she is inside and stare closely before spotting a corner of an ear, a peek of white belly. Discovering Lucero is a much more tricky endeavor. His enclosure is hidden slightly behind Caciora's and just to get a glimpse, one peers between bushes, almost like peeking through the jungle foliage. Lucero is up and walking, stalking back and forth across his enclosure. I would not have been able to notice him at all if it had not been for the motion, so perfectly did his spotted coat blend in with the shadows. One zoo employee tells me how in Lucero's first week in the enclosure this wild born jaguar had already learned how to play peek-a-boo with one of his caretakers. Can you imagine playing a game of hide and shadow with one of these giant killer kitties? This same trainer tells me that when Lucero stares at him, he peers right through him, looking at him differently from the other animals, different even than Caciora, the other jaguar. Maybe this is because Lucero was wild born. He is king of the jungle where he is supposed to live.

On February 17, 2009, the most famous jaguar in the world was captured by accident. Biologists and environmentalists were thrilled when the wild jaguar was fitted with a radio collar before being released. It was hoped that information from the tracking collar would become a valuable tool for revealing secrets of the jaguar. The excitement level heightened when photographs of the captured animal revealed that it was the most famous jaguar in the world, Macho B. Every jaguar has distinctive spots, which can identify him or her as an individual much like human beings and fingerprints. Macho B wore a coat of "Betty Boop" spots.

Macho B was snagged in a snare originally set out for

bears and mountain lions in mountains southwest of Tucson as part of a study about predator travel. Such snares are placed along busy wildlife corridors. When Game and Wildlife officials approached him, Macho B was calm, lying down and resting. He was quickly tranquilized, fitted with a radio collar, and released. The radio collar was designed to transmit a signal every three hours revealing Macho B's location. Game and Fish biologist Bill Van Pelt said "It is like everyday is Easter and we get a new egg every three hours."

When Coronado arrived in Arizona jaguars were found as far north as Utah and as far east as Tennessee. The return of the giant spotted cats to the region has been one of the most exciting environmental stories of recent years.

We know very little about jaguars in Arizona and New Mexico with very few ideas about how Macho B or any jaguar goes about his daily existence in Arizona. What does he eat? Does he rotate territories with seasons? How far does he roam and how far north does he explore? Do wild jaguars interact with each other? It was hoped the radio collar would reveal some answers to these questions. Van Pelt told me the radio collar was designed to emit a special alert every time the big cat crossed the international border with Mexico.

I could not help but giggle. "But the jaguar doesn't care about the border."

Van Pelt laughed, "I suppose that is true."

The euphoria over Macho B's capture and collaring was short lived. Less than two weeks later, radio signals revealed

Macho B was barely moving. Macho B was shot with a tranquilizer dart from a helicopter and taken to the Phoenix Zoo for a veterinarian checkup. The doctor's exam concluded Macho B was experiencing kidney failure. Van Pelt said, "We felt it was in the best interest of the cat to put it down."

Bill Van Pelt said, "It was definitely a roller coaster ride." Interviewing Van Pelt and other Game and Fish officials and hearing the elation in their voices after the jaguar capture, I can only imagine the devastation they felt after the death of the beautiful beast. Conservationists, biologists, nature lovers, and jaguar fans gathered in Tucson to hold a wake for Macho B where Michael Robinson of the Center for Biological Diversity said, "Macho B epitomized the majestic but fragile nature of our southwestern ecosystems. By speaking out for Macho B after he is gone, we fervently hope that our mountains and deserts can still be home to his kin for decades and centuries into the future."

While everyone agrees that the death of Macho B is a tragedy, controversy has arisen over the manner of that death. Some have blamed the trauma from being captured, tranquilized, and collared for the kidney failure. Although some suspected the stress of the capture may have contributed to the kidney failure, Dr. Dean Rice of the Phoenix Zoo said, "I'm sure his kidney was going bad for some time. Kidney's don't go bad at the snap of a finger." "I'm glad they collared him," Rice added. "Otherwise he would have just gone off somewhere and died on his own."

Others claim that Macho B was not an accidental capture at all but was inspired by recent jaguar capture and collars in Northern Mexico. Two of the three jaguar captures in Mexico also resulted in death of the big cats. An autopsy performed by the University of Arizona suggested that Macho B may not have suffered from kidney failure at all but rather from extreme dehydration. The veterinarian suggested that had Macho B received 24 to 48 hours of intravenous fluids he may have recovered. The results of a second autopsy are expected soon, which may confirm or deny the decision to euthanize Macho B. A heated debate which already surrounded the capture and death of Macho B has grown much combative. Some have declared that the loss of a single individual to perpetuate an entire species is a necessary sacrifice.

With the death of Macho B and disappearance of Macho A, opponents of jaguar reintroduction have declared there is no longer proof of any jaguars remaining in Arizona. Although reports of jaguars in the region date back to the conquistadors, Macho B was the first wild jaguar ever captured alive in the United States. The first pictures of living wild jaguars in the United States date back only to 1996 when Warner Glen took his famous video. The unexpected capture of Macho B shows that cameras need to be placed much further north, and that perhaps wild jaguars have penetrated much deeper into North America than anybody has previously realized.

The media frenzy over the capture and death of Macho B has created a flurry of Internet accounts including eyewitness sightings and hearsay. They include a *Los Angeles Times* article about a woman on the edge of the foothills surrounding Tucson reporting a jaguar at her swimming pool before a wildlife official or anyone with a camera could arrive. There are reports of a roadkill jaguar outside of Globe that quickly disappeared and jaguars outside of Wilcox. (If the story about Wilcox jaguars turns out to be true isn't it delightful to imagine them prowling along the shores of the Wilcox playa, the dried up shores where prehistoric Cochise Lake used to be and where saber-toothed cats once prowled along the water's edge a mere 13,000 years ago.) A mountain lion hunter reported seeing the tracks of a jaguar in the snow at Rucker Canyon in the Chiricuahua Mountains in the 1990s. My good friend Barry Wright devoutly maintains that he and some friends spotted a jaguar while hiking in the east unit of Saguaro National Monument during the 1970s. The big, solid black cat growled at them from beneath the shade of a bush as Barry and his friends backed away slowly. Without concrete proof this and other sightings are listed as unconfirmed.

One Internet eyewitness account spoke of an incident in the Mazatzal Wilderness, when a man and his friend saw two jaguars prowling along the riverbank near the confluence of the Verde River and Fossil Creek. This incident took place in 1978 and because the official position of game and wildlife at that time was that jaguars were extinct in this region. The eyewitness account was quickly discounted and dismissed. When one views the record of jaguar sightings in Arizona, going back over the last century, it becomes obvious that there has been a continuous string of sightings every decade. Probably the most famous of these is the jaguar pelt given to Buffalo Bill Cody in Oracle, Arizona on Christmas Day in 1914. Buffalo Bill was given the jaguar pelt, while he was dressed up as Santa Claus. What is most exciting about the Mazatzal sightings (without photographs this still has to be listed as unconfirmed) is the observance of a pair of wild jaguars. As you may have noticed, names such as Macho A and Macho B show that only male jaguars have been photographed so far. Female jaguars will be absolutely essential to a sustainable population in the United States. The last documented female jaguar in Arizona was killed near Big Lake in the White Mountains (not far from where wild wolves were reintroduced) in 1963. In 1898, a female jaguar was shot and killed in the Grand Canyon and it was reported that she had two kittens following her. There is no record at all of what happened to the two kittens or how old they were when their mother was killed. Jaguar kittens remain with the mother for up to two years. Ever since I have heard about the mystery of the missing jaguar kittens in the Grand Canyon the image of giant spotted cats hidden amongst the rugged painted rock and secret oasis of the Grand Canyon has delighted my dreams.

What is it about the return of these wild cats to historic range that excites people?

Aldo Leopold in his essay "Green Lagoons" from his book *Sand County Almanac* describes the Colorado River Delta, "At every shallow ford were tracks of burro deer. We always examined these deer trails, hoping to find signs of the despot of the Delta, the great jaguar, *el Tigre*.

We saw neither hide nor hair of him, but his personality pervaded the wilderness; no living beast forgot his potential presence, for the price of unwariness was death. No deer rounded a bush, or stopped to nibble pods under a mesquite tree, without a premonitory sniff for el Tigre. No campfire died without talk of him. No dog curled up for the night, save at his master's feet; he needed no telling that the king of cats still ruled the night; that those massive paws could fell an ox, those jaws shear off bones like a guillotine.

By this time, the Delta has probably been made safe for cows, and forever dull for adventuring hunters. Freedom from fear has arrived, but a glory has departed from the green lagoons."

The ironic thing about this passage is that the Colorado River Delta which Leopold was writing about, which Leopold described as the most spectacular wilderness he had ever seen, has since disappeared, destroyed by dams, canals, and irrigation; but the jaguar has persevered. The death of Macho B is a tragic loss. It is important that we use the life of Macho B as a rallying point to further conservation efforts, not just to aid the jaguar but also to further bolster the wildness of our wilderness. Game and Fish biologist Bill Van Pelt pointed out that these are exciting times to be an outdoorsman in Arizona – one can see condors soar the northern skies, sing along with wild wolves in the east, and roam the forests of the south alongside the spotted shadows of jaguars.

Historian Frederick Jackson Turner, in his famous paper delivered to the 1898 Chicago World's Fair, announced that it was the frontier, which shaped the American psyche, and that frontier was now closed. It appears to be the aim of conservationists to restore some of that wilderness frontier, to preserve and heal our national soul. The jaguar appears to be the symbol of that return of wildness. I was speaking with my good friend, forest service ranger Duane B. Sapling who wondered out loud if the news reports of "mountains southwest of Tucson" where Macho B was accidentally captured, might not be the Baboquivari's, a range where Macho B was sighted many times over many years. Baboquivari is the sacred peak of the Tohono O'odham peoples and considered to be the home of Elder Brother Iiyotoi. Sapling described Macho B as "Iiyotoi's house cat."

What becomes obvious from research is that jaguars never really left this state; they have been here all along. Now they appear to be returning in stronger numbers than we ever anticipated. Iiyotoi may have lost his favorite house cat but I am certain that Elder Brother sits perched atop Baboquivari Peak guiding other cats into our beautiful home and making sure that our wilderness remains wild, that nature continues to be both glorious and fierce, that a frontier will always exist to shape and heal the soul of future generations of Americans.

I want to stroll the Sendero Pantera
and hunt for jaguar,
discovering a feline Mayan highland prince
and convince him to follow me home
to the Arizona Sonoran Desert
where jaguars once lived,
so that once more the walnut trees
are crowned with fierce growling ghosts
of spot and shadow.

– Gary Every

OhshaD is the Hohokam
word for jaguar.

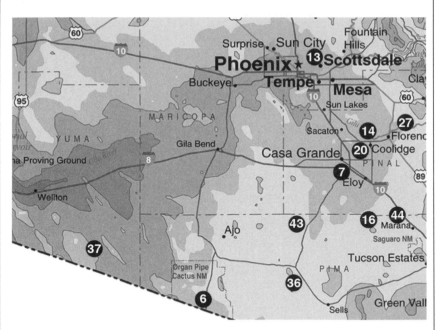

These maps of Arizona (southwest and southeast) will give you an idea of general locations where Gary's stories take place . . .

southwest Arizona:

Ch. 37 .. The Ghost of Melchior Diaz, Raven Butte is located on the
            w. edge of Cabeza Prieta Wildlife Refuge, just n. of Mexico

Ch. 6 ... Ak-Chin Agriculture, Organ Pipe National Monument
            headquarters

Ch. 13 .. Piesetewa Peak (formerly known as Squaw Peak) in Phoenix

Ch. 27 .. Gunfight at the Tunnel Saloon is located in Florence

Ch. 14 .. Japanese Relocation Camps, the closest town is Sacaton

Ch. 20 .. Casa Grande Monument & the Grewe Complex in Coolidge

Ch. 7 ... Lost Treasure of El Tejano, various places including
            Picacho Peak

Ch. 43 .. Ventana Cave, w. of Gu Achi on the Tohono O'odham
            reservation

Ch. 16 .. Ironwood Tree National Monument, w. of Marana

Ch. 44 .. Rillito Roadside Shrine, located off I-10 at Rillito or Marana

Ch. 36 .. The Quijotoa Ghost, located on the O'odham reservation
            in Quijotoa

Arizona Map

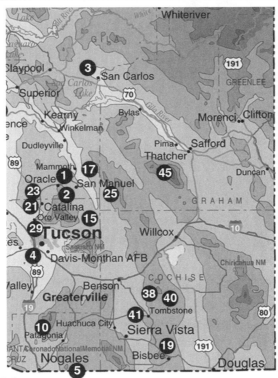

southeast Arizona:

Acknowledgments

First off, I have to mention the love I have for my brothers, sisters, nephews, and nieces; Vickie, David, Kelli, Brandon, Joshua, Delaney, Grace, and Sawyer.

So many people have helped me with this book starting with my hiking buddies Joe Corn, Brian Corn, Barry Wright, Anne Capps, Jeff Mayhew, Scott Burch, Duane B. Sapling, Robert Schulte, Shauna, Samantha, Jerry Orr, Bill Cole, Barbara Michels and many others, all of whom have had to endure my rattling off long and obscure stories about the places we visit.

There are the writers who have inspired and taught me: Henry David Thoreau, John Wesley Powell, John Muir, Aldo Leopold, Emil Haury, Julian Hayden, Ruth Underhill, Ed Abbey, Gary Paul Nabhan, Charles Bowden, Big Jim Griffith, Rochelle Brenner, and many many more.

Thanks to Bob Miles and Bill Van Pelt of Arizona Game and Fish Department for vital information and their photos of Macho B. Thanks to the Huntington family for the photo of Jim. And, of course, this book never would have been possible without the talents and support of Kate Horton and Ellie Mattausch.

Other Books
by Gary Every

"Cat Canyon Secrets"

"Barrio Libre Poems"

"Drunken Astronomers:
  Poems about the Moon and Stars"

"Inca Butterflies: a science fiction novella"

You can contact Gary via email at:
garyevery@gmail.com

Gary Every . . .

Gary Every has won two Arizona Newspaper Awards for best lifestyle feature for *The Apache Naichee Ceremony* and *Losing Geronimos Language*. He has been a four-time nominee for the Rhysling Award for the year's best science fiction poem.

His diverse career paths have included carpenter, chef, piano player, geology explorer, ditch digger, dishwasher, soccer coach, hiking guide, mountain bike instructor, and bonfire storyteller. No doubt while you are reading this, Mr. Every is outdoors somewhere and having a wonderful time.

Gary and his pal "Vixen"

Photo and Art Credits

Photos:

By Gary Every:
Pages 16, 21, 27, 31, 34, 54, 60, 66, 68, 77, 80, 81, 86, 92, 98, 105, 106, 116, 121, 126, 136, 150, 151, 155, 169, 184, 194, 203, 206, 213, 220, 223, 227, 234, 249, back cover

By Arizona Game and Fish Dept.
www.gf.state.az.us/
Macho B – cover, page 242

By Kate Horton:
page 88

By William Cole:
page 261

Jim Huntington photo, page 236
– courtesy of John Huntington & family

Artwork:

By Darrell Klesch
Page 56

By Kate Horton
Pages 122, 130

By Jerry Parra,
www.jerryparra.com
Cody metal cutout, page 151

Shadow of the OhshaD

The stories in this book were published in *The Oracle* newspaper. It is a monthly publication with many feature stories and articles by outstanding writers.

If you want to read the most recent of Gary Every's stories and poems, subscribe to *The Oracle*. A year's subscription is $22. Send a check with your name and address to HC1 Box 2361, Oracle, Arizona 85623.

Copies of *The Shadow of the OhshaD* are also available by sending $20 per copy (postpaid) to the above address.

– Ellie Mattausch
Editor and publisher of
The Oracle